Micro Investing Mastery

Grow Big Money with Spare Change

ETHAN WEALTHMORE

Table of Contents

Chapter 1: Investing Is for Everyone

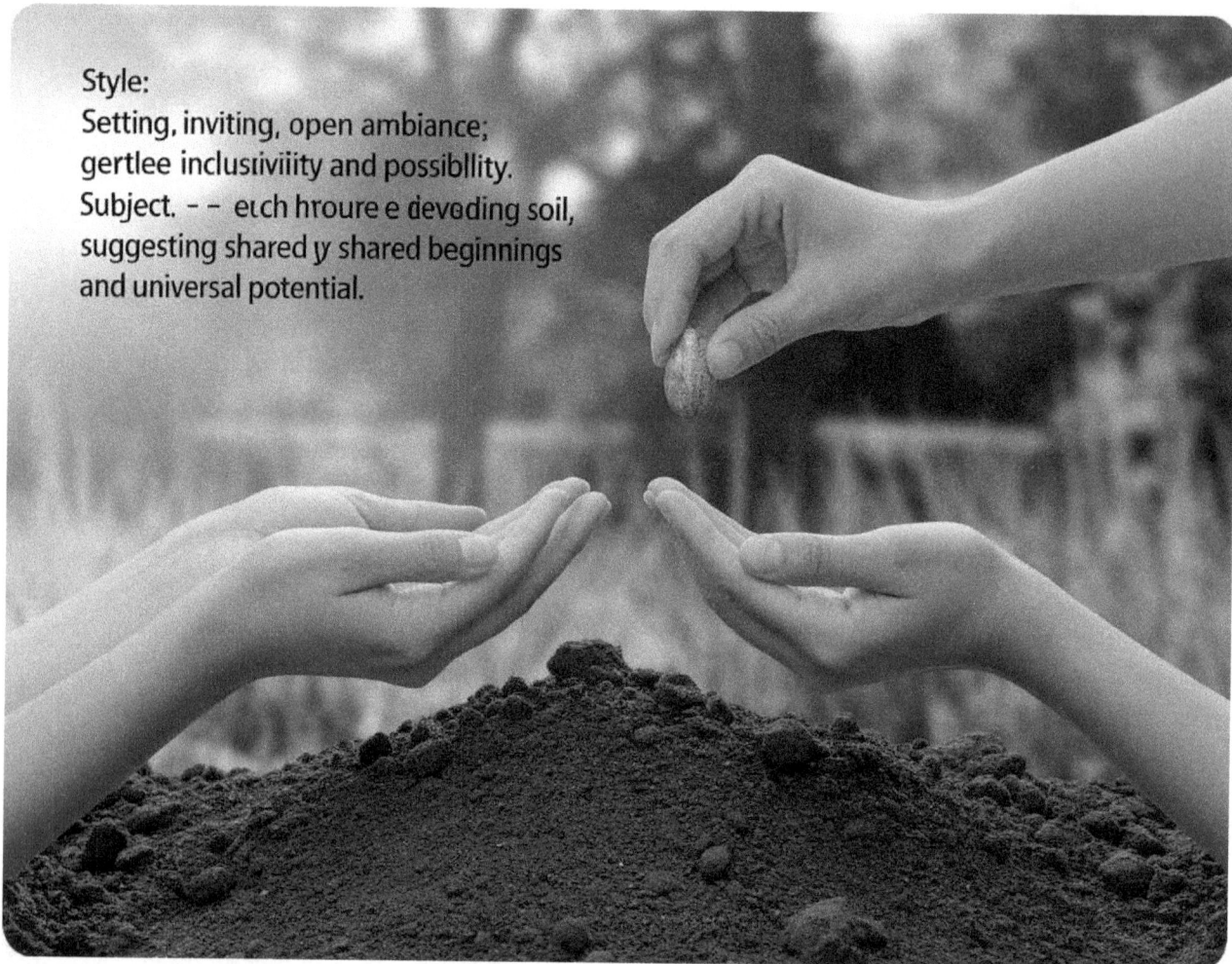

Style:
Setting, inviting, open ambiance;
gentle inclusivity and possibility.
Subject. - - each hroure e devoding soil,
suggesting shared y shared beginnings
and universal potential.

Tip

If you're feeling overwhelmed by financial jargon or the fear of losing money, start small and focus on learning as you go. Use beginner-friendly apps like Acorns or Stash to invest spare change, and take advantage of the free educational resources most platforms offer. Remember, consistency and patience matter more than the size of your first investment. Building wealth is a journey—take your first step today, no matter how small.

In recent years, investing has transformed significantly, welcoming individuals from all walks of life to participate. Thanks to technology, more people can access opportunities, allowing even those without substantial funds or extensive market knowledge to begin their journey toward building wealth. Now, anyone with internet access can explore a variety of tools and platforms, making it easier to start accumulating assets with just a small amount of capital.

This shift toward more accessible investing is largely driven by the emergence of online brokerages, mobile apps, and **robo-advisors**. These innovations have lowered the barriers to entry, enabling individuals to invest without relying on traditional financial advisors. Young adults, in particular, are reaping the benefits of these changes, as they seek to take charge of their financial futures but may feel daunted by the stock market or think they need a significant amount of money to get started.

Online brokerages have been instrumental in this evolution. Companies like **Robinhood**, **E*TRADE**, and **Charles Schwab** have simplified the process for beginners to open accounts and start investing. These platforms often feature low or zero commission fees, allowing users to buy and sell stocks without the worry of high transaction costs diminishing their returns. This is especially beneficial for those new to investing who want to experiment with smaller investments without incurring hefty fees.

The design of these platforms is also tailored to novices. Their user-friendly interfaces include intuitive dashboards that help users track their investments, review market trends, and make decisions with confidence. *Robinhood*, for instance, is celebrated for its clean layout and easy navigation, which resonates with younger investors who value straightforward, simple tools.

Mobile apps have also played a significant role in making investing more accessible. Applications like **Acorns** and **Stash** have introduced innovative ways for people to invest spare change or small amounts of money regularly. *Acorns*, for example, rounds up everyday purchases to the nearest dollar and invests the difference in a diversified portfolio. This approach allows individuals to gradually grow their wealth without the pressure of making large, one-time investments.

Robo-advisors have further broadened access to investing. These services utilize algorithms to manage portfolios based on each person's risk tolerance and financial goals. Companies such as **Betterment** and **Wealthfront** offer robo-advisory services that are both affordable and efficient, reducing costs and making professional management available to a much wider audience, regardless of their financial background.

These digital tools stand out because they cater to the needs of new investors. They provide educational resources—like articles, videos, and tutorials—that help users grasp the basics of investing and make informed decisions. Learning these fundamentals is essential for building confidence and overcoming the apprehension that often holds beginners back.

A common misconception about investing is that you need a large sum of money to get started, which can often discourage people, especially those who are just beginning to manage their finances.

Micro Investing Mastery

The truth is, investing isn't just for the wealthy or those with extensive financial knowledge. Many successful investors began with small amounts and gradually built their wealth over time.

Micro-investing has gained popularity in recent years, enabling individuals to contribute small amounts—sometimes as little as $5—into a diversified portfolio through various platforms. This approach is particularly appealing to young adults who may not have much to invest at the outset. Research indicates that even small, regular contributions can add up significantly over time, thanks to the power of **compound interest**. For example, setting aside just $5 a day with an average annual return of 7% can grow to more than $76,000 in 20 years. This example shows that building wealth relies more on consistency and time than on the size of the initial investment.

Compound interest is essential for investment growth, as it generates earnings on both the original amount and the accumulated interest. Starting early gives your money more time to flourish. The **compound interest formula**, $A = P(1 + r/n)^{nt}$, calculates the total amount after n years, where P is the initial sum, r is the annual interest rate as a decimal, n is the number of times interest is compounded per year, and t is the number of years. This formula illustrates how even small investments can grow significantly over time.

Stories of real investors who began with modest sums challenge the notion that you need substantial wealth to start. Consider the following examples:

- Grace Groner, who worked as a secretary, invested $180 in her company's stock in 1935. Over the decades, her investment grew to more than $7 million by the time she passed away in 2010. Her journey demonstrates that patience and a long-term perspective can transform a small start into considerable wealth.
- Ronald Read, a janitor and gas station attendant, built an $8 million fortune through careful spending and smart investing. He focused on purchasing blue-chip stocks and holding them for the long term. His story shows that you don't need extensive financial expertise to succeed. With discipline and a commitment to long-term growth, impressive results are within reach.

Fear of losing money is one of the most significant psychological barriers that can hold people back from starting their investment journey. This anxiety often arises from the perception that investing is akin to gambling, where the risk of losing everything feels daunting. However, investing is really about making thoughtful, calculated decisions to build wealth over time, rather than taking reckless risks. A practical way to ease this fear is to begin with small, manageable investments. By allocating just a small portion of your savings—like **5%**—to your first investments, you can get a feel for how the market operates without putting a large part of your finances at risk. This approach allows you to learn and adapt in a low-risk environment, helping to reduce the anxiety associated with the possibility of significant losses.

Micro Investing Mastery

A lack of financial literacy is another common hurdle. Many individuals think they need extensive expertise to succeed, which can feel overwhelming. In reality, you don't need a formal education in finance to start investing. Today's investment platforms provide a wealth of educational materials tailored for beginners, including:

- Articles
- Videos
- Live webinars
- Interactive courses

These resources break down the basics of the stock market and financial statements. Taking advantage of them helps you gradually build your knowledge and confidence, making it easier to take that first step.

Financial jargon can also be a barrier, making participation in the market feel daunting. Terms like *dividends, bull market,* and *asset allocation* may seem complex at first. Simplifying these concepts can make a big difference. For example, **dividends** are simply a way for companies to share some of their profits with shareholders, while a **bull market** refers to a time when stock prices are generally on the rise. Clarifying these ideas can make investing feel less intimidating and more approachable.

Online communities and forums provide another wonderful way to overcome psychological barriers. These spaces allow beginners to share experiences, ask questions, and learn from others who are navigating similar challenges. Connecting with individuals who share your interests offers support, encouragement, and practical advice. Hearing about the successes of others who started with small investments can be especially motivating and reassuring.

Think of investing as a skill that develops over time, rather than a one-time event. Like any skill, it requires practice and patience. Starting early, even with small amounts, gives you the opportunity to learn and grow gradually. The sooner you begin, the more time you have to recover from mistakes and benefit from the compounding effect of your investments. The goal isn't to become an expert overnight, but to steadily build your knowledge and confidence along the way.

Setting realistic financial goals is the cornerstone of a strong investment strategy. Begin by taking a close look at your current financial situation, which includes a detailed analysis of your monthly income, fixed and variable expenses, outstanding debts, and current savings. This evaluation will help you identify the maximum amount you can invest each month while still covering your essential living expenses. With a clear understanding of your finances, you can establish specific, measurable, achievable, relevant, and time-bound (**SMART**) goals. For instance, you might set a goal to save $50,000 for a house down payment within five years or to build an emergency fund that covers six months of essential living expenses, estimated at $3,000 per month.

A personalized investment plan should align your financial objectives with your risk tolerance and investment time horizon. Your risk tolerance reflects how much market volatility you can comfortably manage. If you prefer a more cautious approach, a conservative portfolio with a higher proportion of fixed-income securities like bonds or stable dividend-paying stocks may be a good fit, as these typically offer lower but more predictable returns. On the other hand, if you're open to taking on more risk, a portfolio with a larger share of equities could be suitable, since stocks have historically provided higher potential returns over longer periods. The length of time you plan to keep your money invested before needing it—your investment horizon—also influences your strategy. Longer horizons, such as 10 years or more, generally support more aggressive investment approaches and allow time to recover from market downturns.

Diversification is essential for managing investment risk. By spreading your investments across different asset classes—such as equities, fixed-income securities, and real estate—you can reduce the impact of any single investment's poor performance on your overall portfolio. Even with limited capital, you can achieve diversification through investment vehicles like exchange-traded funds (*ETFs*) and fractional shares. ETFs trade on stock exchanges like individual stocks and typically hold a diversified portfolio of assets, giving you exposure to a broad market index or specific sector with just one purchase. Fractional shares allow you to buy a portion of a stock, making it possible to invest in high-priced stocks without needing a large initial investment.

To gain a clear view of your financial situation and set achievable objectives, closely track your income and expenses using budgeting tools or financial management apps. This process can help you identify areas where you might cut spending and redirect those funds toward your investment goals. After creating a budget, define your short-term, medium-term, and long-term objectives:

- Short-term goals might include saving $2,000 for a vacation or a new electronic device.
- Medium-term goals could involve accumulating $15,000 for a vehicle or funding a $10,000 education program.
- Long-term goals often focus on retirement savings, such as building a $1 million nest egg or purchasing a home valued at $300,000.

Regularly reviewing your progress is key to staying on track with your investment plan. Take the time to check your portfolio's performance and make adjustments as needed. This could mean rebalancing to maintain your target asset allocation or increasing contributions as your financial situation improves. Many investment platforms offer analytical tools and performance reports to help you track your progress and make informed decisions.

Chapter 2: Debunking Myths About Small-Amount Investing

Tip

Start small and stay consistent. Even if you can only invest $10 or $20 a month, regular contributions add up thanks to compound interest. Use automatic transfers or round-up features on digital platforms to make investing effortless. Over time, these small steps can lead to significant growth and help you build confidence as a new investor. Remember, it's not about how much you start with, but how often you invest and how long you let your money grow.

One of the most common myths about investing is the idea that it's an exclusive activity meant only for those with significant wealth. This misconception can be disheartening, especially for young adults who are just starting to navigate their financial responsibilities. The reality is that the amount of your initial capital doesn't dictate your ability to invest. What truly matters is **consistency** and **time**, as even small, regular contributions can grow into substantial sums over the years, largely due to the power of **compound interest**.

This principle is essential for nurturing your investments over the long haul. It works by generating earnings not just on your initial investment but also on the interest that has already been earned. For instance, the formula for compound interest is:

$$A = P(1 + r/n)^{nt}$$

In this equation, A represents the total amount accumulated after n years, including interest. P is the principal amount (your initial investment), r is the annual interest rate expressed as a decimal, n is how often interest is compounded each year, and t is the number of years your money is invested.

Imagine starting with $100 and adding $10 each month. With an average annual return of 7% compounded monthly, your investment could grow to over $8,000 in 20 years. This example illustrates how modest, consistent contributions can lead to impressive growth over time, effectively debunking the notion that small investments don't matter.

Another common belief is that investing requires a deep understanding of complex financial markets. While having knowledge is beneficial, modern digital tools have simplified the process significantly. Beginners can now dive in without needing to become financial experts. Platforms like Acorns and Stash provide features such as:

- Automatic investment plans
- Round-up programs
- User-friendly interfaces

These tools make investing straightforward and accessible for anyone with a smartphone and a bank account.

Automatic investment plans are particularly helpful for those who may not have large sums to invest all at once. By setting up a plan to transfer a fixed amount from your checking account to your investment account each month, you can gradually build your portfolio without needing constant oversight. This method encourages disciplined saving and employs **dollar-cost averaging**—a strategy where you invest a set amount regularly, regardless of market conditions. This can help mitigate the effects of market volatility on your investments over time.

Round-up programs further simplify investing by rounding up purchases to the nearest dollar and investing the difference. For example, if you buy a coffee for $2.75, it rounds up to $3.00, and the extra $0.25 gets invested. These small amounts can accumulate quickly, especially if you make numerous transactions each month.

Digital tools like these have significantly enhanced the accessibility of investing. They eliminate barriers that once kept many people from entering the market, such as high minimum investment requirements and complicated processes. Micro-investing platforms now empower individuals to take charge of their financial futures, regardless of how much money they start with.

Many platforms also provide educational resources to help beginners grasp the basics of investing. These resources may include articles, videos, and interactive tutorials that explain key concepts in an easy-to-understand manner. Engaging with these materials can boost your financial literacy and instill the confidence needed to make informed investment decisions.

Many beginners see investing as overly complex or too risky, but a structured approach can help ease these concerns. Start by opening a basic investment account through user-friendly platforms designed for newcomers, such as **Robinhood, E*TRADE**, or **Acorns**. These services guide you through the account setup process, typically asking for a few personal details and a linked bank account to get you started.

Once your account is set up, take some time to explore options that offer easy diversification. **Exchange-traded funds (ETFs)** and **index funds** are great choices for those new to investing. These funds pool money from many investors to buy a broad mix of stocks or bonds, which helps spread out risk. For example, an *S&P 500* index fund invests in the 500 largest publicly traded U.S. companies, providing wide market exposure and reducing the impact of any single stock's poor performance on your overall portfolio.

When selecting an ETF or index fund, pay attention to important details like the **expense ratio**— the annual fee as a percentage of your investment. Lower expense ratios mean more of your money stays invested. It's also wise to review the fund's past performance and the sectors it covers to ensure it aligns with your goals and comfort with risk.

Starting with a small investment is a smart way to build confidence and reduce perceived risk. Consider putting in a modest amount, such as $50 or $100, to familiarize yourself with how investing works. This approach allows you to learn about market movements without the stress of losing a large sum. As you gain experience and feel more comfortable, you can gradually increase your investment.

Taking that first step is crucial. Making regular, small contributions can lead to significant financial growth over time thanks to **compound interest**. Even minimal, consistent investments can make a big difference; for example, contributing $100 each month with an average annual return of 7% can grow to over $24,000 in ten years.

Staying motivated is key to sticking with your investment plan. Setting short-term goals can help you feel accomplished and engaged. For instance, aim to:

- Save a certain amount in the first six months
- Reach a specific portfolio value by the end of the year
- Track your progress regularly

These smaller targets help you work toward your larger financial objectives.

Investment platforms often include tools to track your progress, set alerts for market changes, and visualize your portfolio's growth. Seeing your results in real time can boost motivation and reinforce the benefits of steady investing.

Celebrating small wins along the way is important, too. Whether you hit a savings goal, see a positive return, or stick to your plan for a set period, acknowledging these achievements can build your confidence and help you stay committed.

Overcoming the Fear of Limited Funds

Starting your investment journey with limited funds can feel a bit daunting, but it's essential to embrace the idea that any amount, no matter how small, is a wonderful way to begin. Investing isn't just for the wealthy; it's a financial tool available to anyone who is ready to take that first step. Many successful investors started with very little, showing us that your initial amount doesn't dictate your future financial growth.

Take Grace Groner, for instance. She invested just $180 in her company's stock back in 1935, and over the years, that investment blossomed into more than $7 million. Her story beautifully illustrates how patience and a long-term perspective can transform a modest sum into significant wealth. Ronald Read, who worked as a janitor and gas station attendant, built an impressive $8 million fortune by spending wisely and investing thoughtfully. His journey highlights that consistent effort and a focus on long-term growth can yield remarkable results, no matter where you start.

Micro-investing platforms and apps have made it easier than ever to get started, even if you only have a few dollars to spare. Services like **Acorns** and **Stash** are designed for those with limited funds, offering features such as:

- Automatic investment plans
- Round-up programs that simplify the process
- Options to invest spare change from everyday purchases

These apps allow you to round up everyday purchases to the nearest dollar and invest that spare change, helping you gradually grow your wealth without the pressure of making large, one-time investments.

Setting up an account on these platforms is a breeze. You'll typically need to provide some personal information and link your bank account. Once you're all set up, you can take advantage of features like **fractional shares**, which let you buy a piece of expensive stocks without needing to purchase a whole share. This means you can own part of companies like *Amazon* or *Google*, even if a full share is beyond your reach. Fractional shares make the stock market accessible to individuals in a variety of financial situations.

Establishing realistic financial goals that align with your personal circumstances is crucial. Investing doesn't require a hefty upfront sum. Start by reviewing your income, expenses, and savings to see how much you can comfortably invest each month. Creating a simple budget with a small, regular investment amount helps you build discipline and good habits over time. Even setting aside $20 a month can add up, thanks to the magic of **compound interest**.

Investment platforms often offer educational resources like tutorials, webinars, and articles that break down complex topics into easy-to-understand information. Taking advantage of these resources empowers you to make informed choices and navigate the investment world with greater confidence. Keeping an eye on market trends and your own investments is also important, as it allows you to make smart decisions and adapt to changes in the market.

Real-Life Stories of Small-Scale Investors

In the bustling corridors of a university campus, Sarah, a college sophomore, found herself juggling a heavy load of textbooks alongside her part-time jobs. With tuition fees exceeding **$10,000** annually, the thought of investing felt like a distant dream. Then she discovered a micro-investing app that promised to transform her spare change into a growing portfolio. Intrigued by its potential, Sarah decided to give it a shot. Each time she bought a coffee or a snack, the app rounded up her transactions to the nearest dollar and invested the difference, usually around **$0.50** per purchase. While her friends were skeptical about the impact of these small amounts and dismissed her efforts, she was determined to see what these contributions could achieve.

As she faced her share of challenges, Sarah often wondered if these tiny investments would ever amount to something significant. Nevertheless, she set up automatic transfers of **$5** each week into her investment account and remained committed to her plan. Over time, she began to witness the effects of **compound interest** as her small contributions started to grow. This progress inspired her to delve deeper into finance, prompting her to read articles and watch educational videos offered by the app. As her knowledge expanded, so did her confidence, shifting her initial goal of saving for a post-graduation trip toward building a **financial safety net** for her future.

Meanwhile, across town, Jake, a young professional who had just completed college, was embarking on his career journey. With his first paycheck of about **$3,000**, he was eager to invest but unsure where to start. He opted to buy fractional shares instead of whole shares of pricier stocks. By setting aside **$100** from his monthly paycheck, he could invest in companies he admired, like *Apple* and *Tesla*, without straining his budget. His strategy was straightforward: automate investments and allow them to grow over time.

Jake's friends were doubtful, preferring to spend their money on immediate pleasures rather than planning for the future. He remained focused, believing that even small investments could lead to meaningful returns. By joining online forums and communities, he learned from seasoned investors and gained valuable insights about market trends and strategies. As his portfolio expanded, so did his aspirations. What began as a way to save for a new laptop evolved into a plan to buy his first home, with a goal of saving **$50,000**.

In another part of the city, Maria, a single parent, was determined to create a brighter future for her child. With a monthly budget of **$2,500**, she understood the importance of a thoughtful investment plan. She started by setting aside **$100** each month and carefully managed her expenses to ensure she could keep contributing. Maria built a diverse portfolio with a mix of stocks and bonds, utilizing digital tools to track her progress and make adjustments as needed.

Navigating unexpected expenses and the constant demands of parenthood, Maria remained focused on her financial goals. The vision of building a legacy for her child kept her motivated. Over time, her investments flourished through compounding, and she watched her portfolio steadily increase. Her journey illustrates how determination and adaptability can lead to genuine financial progress, even when resources are limited.

Chapter 3: Building Wealth by Starting Small

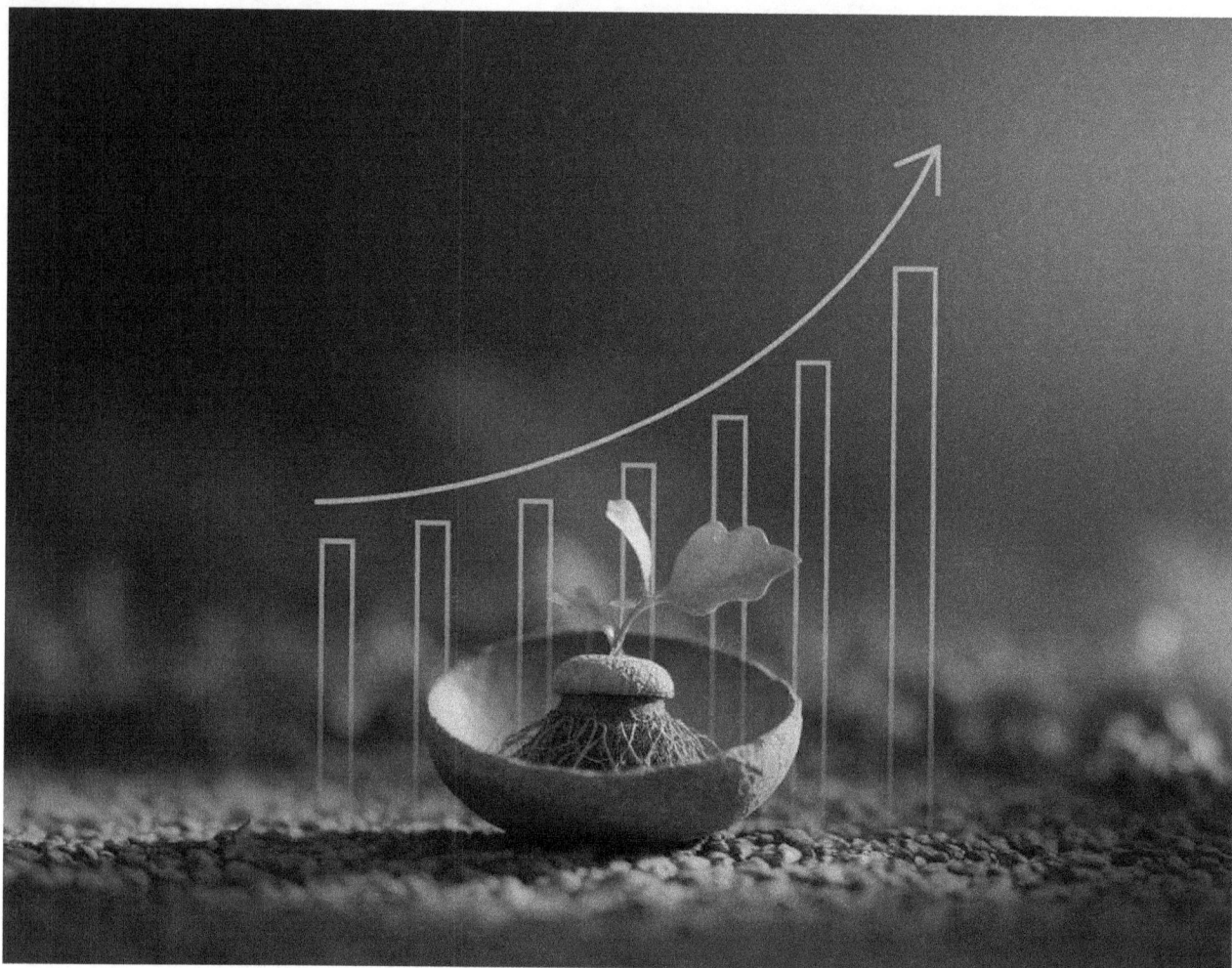

Investing small amounts isn't just practical; it's a powerful strategy that lays the foundation for building wealth over time. **Micro-investing** offers both psychological and financial benefits, making it accessible and empowering for everyone. Starting with modest contributions allows for steady growth of your financial base without the pressure of large, upfront commitments.

The magic of **compounding** plays a vital role in making these investments effective. Compounding means your earnings begin to generate their own returns, so even minor, regular contributions can grow significantly over the years. For example, investing $50 each month at a 7% annual return could lead to more than $60,000 after 30 years. This growth stems from both your original contributions and the interest earned on previous gains, which accelerates your overall progress.

Building a disciplined savings habit from the start is another wonderful benefit of beginning small. Setting aside a portion of your income for investments fosters financial responsibility and discipline.

This approach not only supports wealth accumulation but also provides a greater sense of control over your finances. Regular, small investments can help you achieve important goals, such as:

- Buying a home
- Funding education
- Securing a comfortable retirement

Starting with limited funds helps minimize the risks associated with investing. Smaller amounts allow you to learn and refine your strategies without exposing yourself to significant financial loss. This early stage is crucial for understanding market trends, experimenting with different methods, and making adjustments based on real experiences. Lower risk makes it easier to recover from mistakes and builds confidence in your decision-making.

Digital tools and platforms have revolutionized how individuals with limited resources can engage in the market. **Micro-investing apps** and online platforms have made it accessible to almost anyone, even with just a few dollars. Many of these resources offer educational materials to help you make informed choices and enhance your financial knowledge. They enable you to track investments, set goals, and adjust strategies to maximize growth.

A focus on **financial literacy** and responsibility develops as you witness your investments grow, even in small increments. Observing your progress can boost motivation and confidence, which are essential for continuing to invest and expanding your knowledge. Achieving smaller goals can be incredibly encouraging and can propel you toward larger financial targets.

To get the most out of small investments, set realistic goals and keep an eye on your progress. Start by reviewing your finances to determine how much you can invest each month. Utilize budgeting tools to track income and expenses, ensuring your investment plan remains sustainable. Regularly check your portfolio's performance and make adjustments as needed to stay aligned with your financial objectives.

Chapter 4: Smart Investing Basics for Beginners

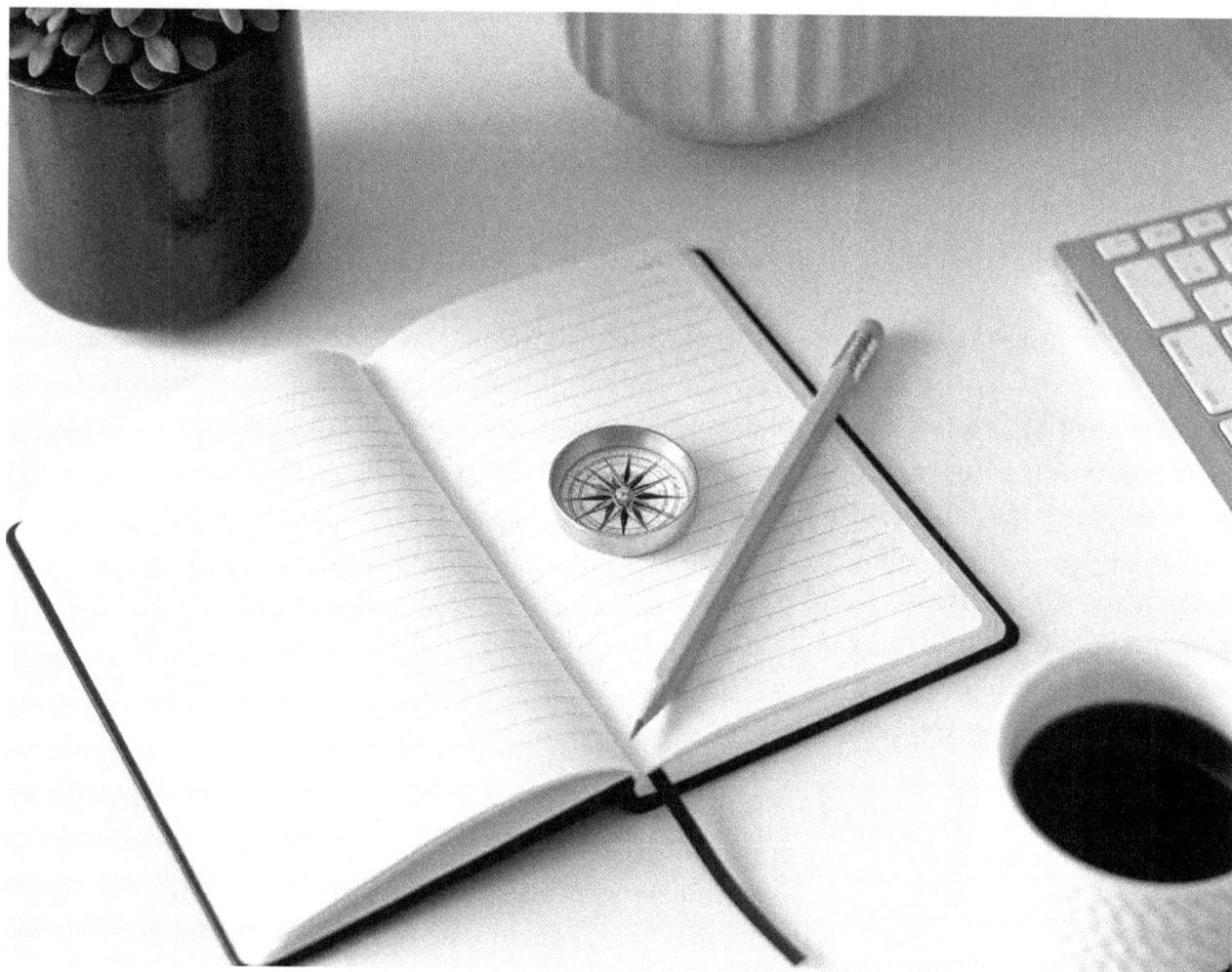

Tip

Feeling overwhelmed by all the investment options? Start small and focus on learning as you go. You don't need to master every vehicle at once—choose one or two that match your goals and risk comfort, then gradually expand your knowledge. Consistency and curiosity are your best allies as you build confidence and grow your wealth.

Entering the world of investing can feel a bit daunting with so many options available, but getting to know the different types of investment vehicles is essential for making informed choices. Let's explore some of the most common options for beginners: **stocks**, **bonds**, **mutual funds**, **ETFs**, and **real estate**.

Stocks represent a piece of ownership in a company. When you buy a stock, you own a small part of that company and are entitled to a share of its profits and assets. They can offer high returns, but they also come with greater risk since their value can change significantly based on the company's performance and market conditions. For example, strong earnings reports can boost a stock's price and lead to a profit when you sell, while disappointing results can cause a decline in value.

Bonds work a bit differently. They are essentially loans made to corporations or governments, and in return, you receive regular interest payments and get your principal back when the bond matures. Generally considered safer than stocks, bonds provide more predictable returns, although potential gains are often lower. The main risk lies in whether the issuer can repay what they owe. Government bonds are typically safer than corporate ones, but they usually offer lower interest rates.

Mutual funds gather money from many investors to create a diversified portfolio of stocks, bonds, or other securities. This strategy helps reduce risk because the fund's performance isn't reliant on just one investment. Professional managers oversee these funds, which can be a great option for beginners looking for a more hands-off approach. However, keep in mind that management fees can eat into your returns.

Exchange-Traded Funds (ETFs) also offer diversification by holding a mix of different securities, but they trade on stock exchanges like individual stocks. This structure provides more flexibility for buying and selling. ETFs often have lower fees than mutual funds, making them appealing for those who want to keep costs down. Many track specific indices, sectors, or commodities, allowing you to align your investments with your interests and goals.

Real estate involves purchasing property to generate income or benefit from rising values. This can include residential homes, commercial buildings, or undeveloped land. It can provide steady income through rent and may offer tax benefits, but it requires a significant upfront investment and carries risks like property value declines or tenant issues. **Real Estate Investment Trusts (REITs)** allow you to invest in real estate without direct ownership, giving you access to the market while maintaining the liquidity of stocks.

Learning about these investment vehicles is just the start. Managing risk is equally important, and **diversification** is a key strategy. Spreading investments across different asset classes helps mitigate risk. By avoiding concentration in one area, a loss in one sector won't impact your entire portfolio as severely. For instance, if stocks aren't performing well, gains in bonds or real estate might help balance things out.

Asset allocation is another important concept. This involves dividing investments among different asset classes based on your risk tolerance and financial goals. A younger investor with more time might allocate more funds to stocks for higher growth, while someone nearing retirement may prefer a safer mix with more bonds. Ensuring that your asset allocation aligns with your risk tolerance and investment objectives is essential.

Market volatility refers to the fluctuations in investment prices, and it's a normal part of investing. Understanding how volatility works can empower you to make informed decisions and avoid panic during market downturns. While it can be unsettling, it can also present opportunities to buy investments at lower prices. Staying informed about market trends and maintaining a long-term perspective can help you navigate these ups and downs with confidence.

A strategic investment plan starts with clearly identifying your specific financial goals, which can be grouped into **short-term**, **medium-term**, and **long-term** objectives.

- Short-term aims might include saving for a vacation or purchasing a new electronic device, typically within a one to three-year timeframe.
- Medium-term objectives, such as buying a vehicle or funding further education, generally span three to five years.
- Long-term aspirations, like saving for retirement or acquiring a home, extend beyond five years.

By defining these targets, you can better assess your risk tolerance and choose the investment options that suit you best.

Once you've established your goals, the next step is to create a detailed investment budget. This process involves taking a close look at your current financial situation, including your income, fixed and variable expenses, and existing savings. The *50/30/20 rule* provides a helpful budgeting framework: allocate 50% of your income to essentials, 30% to discretionary spending, and 20% to savings and investments. Feel free to adjust this rule to better fit your personal circumstances. The important thing is to ensure that your investment contributions remain consistent and manageable over time.

Distributing funds among various investment vehicles helps balance risk and potential returns. This allocation should align with your risk tolerance, reflecting how comfortable you are with market fluctuations. For example, if you have a higher risk tolerance, you might choose to invest more in **equities**, which can offer higher returns but also come with increased volatility. If you prefer a more stable approach, focusing on **bonds** or other fixed-income securities may be a better fit for you.

A *dollar-cost averaging* strategy is a great way to navigate market volatility. By investing a set amount of money at regular intervals, regardless of market conditions, you can reduce the impact of price swings. This means buying more shares when prices are low and fewer when prices are high.

Over time, this can help lower the average cost per share and potentially enhance your overall returns.

Staying informed about market trends and economic indicators is essential for making well-informed investment choices. Economic data such as **GDP growth**, **unemployment rates**, and **inflation figures** provide valuable context about the broader economy and can influence market performance. Keeping up with financial news, investment newsletters, and insights from reputable analysts helps you stay aware. Many investment platforms also offer analytical tools and resources to help you track trends and assess economic data.

Regularly reviewing and updating your investment plan ensures it remains aligned with your evolving financial goals and current market conditions. Major life events like a job change, marriage, or the birth of a child can significantly impact your financial situation and objectives. Additionally, changes in the market may require you to reassess your risk tolerance and asset allocation. It's a good idea to review your investment plan at least once a year or after any major life event.

Financial literacy is the cornerstone of successful investing, especially for those just starting out. It encompasses understanding essential concepts like **risk assessment**, **expected returns**, **diversification strategies**, and how economic indicators such as *interest rates* and *inflation* can influence investment outcomes. To enhance your financial knowledge, explore a variety of resources. For instance, *"The Intelligent Investor"* by Benjamin Graham delves into the principles of value investing, while *"A Random Walk Down Wall Street"* by Burton Malkiel examines various strategies, including index investing and behavioral finance. Online courses from platforms like Coursera or Khan Academy offer structured lessons that cater to everyone, from beginners to advanced learners.

Staying informed through reputable financial news sources is vital. Consider the following outlets:

- Bloomberg
- CNBC
- The Wall Street Journal

These sources provide timely updates on market trends, economic changes, and company performance, empowering you to make informed decisions. Additionally, finance-focused podcasts and YouTube channels present information in engaging formats, making it easier to learn while you go about your daily activities.

Emotions significantly influence investment decisions and can sometimes lead to choices that deviate from sound strategies. Common psychological biases, such as **loss aversion**, may prompt investors to sell too quickly during downturns, while **overconfidence** can lead to taking on excessive risk without thorough analysis. Building emotional resilience is key to countering these biases. By adopting a long-term perspective and concentrating on your financial goals, rather than reacting to short-term market fluctuations, you can avoid impulsive decisions driven by temporary conditions.

Establishing clear investment rules or guidelines and committing to them, regardless of market changes, is another effective strategy. This could involve setting specific criteria for buying or selling assets, such as:

- A target price
- A predetermined percentage change in value
- A specific time frame for holding investments

Adhering to these rules can help minimize the emotional impact on your decisions.

Becoming part of investment communities, both online and in person, can provide valuable support and insights. Platforms like *Reddit's r/investing* or forums such as *Bogleheads* create spaces for sharing experiences, asking questions, and learning from seasoned investors. Connecting with others who share your financial aspirations can also enhance motivation and accountability.

Patience and discipline are crucial for building wealth. Investing is not a quick route to riches; it requires ongoing effort and a willingness to learn from both successes and setbacks. Setting realistic goals and focusing on steady progress can help you steer clear of the pitfalls associated with chasing quick returns or making hasty decisions in response to market changes.

Regularly reviewing your investment plan and making adjustments as necessary is important. Changes in your life or financial goals may require you to update your strategy. This continuous process of evaluation and adaptation ensures that your investments remain aligned with your objectives and risk tolerance.

Understanding Risk and Reward for New Investors

In the world of investing, grasping the intricate relationship between **risk** and **reward** is essential for making informed decisions. Risk refers to the possibility of financial loss or the unpredictability of investment returns, which means that whenever you invest money, there's always a chance your investment could lose value and lead to a financial setback. On the flip side, reward represents the potential for profit or positive returns, which can manifest as capital gains, dividends, or interest payments.

These two concepts are closely intertwined. Investments that present the opportunity for higher returns typically come with greater risk. This connection exists because achieving substantial returns often involves embracing more uncertainty. For example, investing in a startup could yield impressive gains if the business flourishes, but there's also a significant risk of losing your entire investment if the company doesn't succeed. In contrast, investing in government bonds generally offers lower returns, but the risk is much lower since defaults are quite rare.

To illustrate the risk-reward trade-off, consider the following formula:

$$\text{Expected Return} = \text{Risk-Free Rate} + \text{Risk Premium}$$

In this equation, the **risk-free rate** represents the return from an investment with minimal risk, such as a U.S. Treasury bond. The **risk premium** is the additional return expected for taking on extra risk. A higher risk premium suggests the potential for greater rewards, but it also indicates increased risk.

Understanding your own **risk tolerance** is a vital part of investing. This tolerance reflects the level of risk you're comfortable taking to achieve your financial goals. It varies from person to person and is influenced by factors such as age, income, financial objectives, and your comfort level with uncertainty. For instance, a young individual with a steady income and a long investment horizon might be more inclined to take on additional risk and invest more heavily in stocks, which can be volatile but offer higher potential returns. Conversely, someone approaching retirement may prefer safer investments like bonds to safeguard their savings.

Begin by assessing your financial situation—your income, expenses, savings, and any current investments—to determine how much risk you can reasonably manage. Next, reflect on your knowledge of different types of investments and the risks they entail, as being well-informed can empower you to make better choices. It's also important to consider how you might emotionally respond to losses, as investing can be stressful, and being prepared for market fluctuations is key.

Regularly reviewing your financial status, investment knowledge, and emotional readiness helps keep your risk assessment current. Maintaining this ongoing process ensures your investment strategy aligns with your risk tolerance and financial goals. By taking this proactive approach, you enhance your decision-making and build confidence, knowing that your investments resonate with your comfort level.

To illustrate the **risk-reward** relationship, let's explore some examples that resonate with small-scale investors. Take stocks, for instance. These investments are often described as **high-risk, high-reward**. Investing in a technology company like Apple or Tesla has, in the past, led to remarkable growth and substantial returns for those who got in early. A $1,000 investment in Apple back in 2000 would have blossomed to over $100,000 by 2023, resulting in an annualized return of about 18%. This impressive growth came with its share of ups and downs, as stock prices can fluctuate by 20% or more in a single year due to market sentiment, company earnings, or broader economic factors. Such variations mean investors face the potential for both significant gains and notable losses.

Bonds, on the other hand, typically provide a more stable investment with lower risk and potential returns. When you purchase a bond, you're essentially lending money to a corporation or government, which promises to repay the principal plus interest over a specified period. U.S. Treasury bonds, for example, are regarded as some of the safest investments because they are backed by the federal government. These usually yield an average annual return of 2-3%, and the risk of losing your principal is quite low. This makes them appealing for those seeking steady income with less exposure to risk.

Mutual funds and ETFs offer a wonderful way for investors to achieve diversification, balancing risk and reward. These vehicles pool money from many individuals to create a portfolio of stocks, bonds, or other securities. A mutual fund might spread its assets across:

- large-cap stocks
- small-cap stocks
- bonds

This strategy can lead to moderate returns with less volatility than investing in individual stocks. ETFs, which trade on exchanges like stocks, provide similar diversification but often come with lower expense ratios, making them a smart choice for cost-conscious investors.

Imagine putting a small amount of money into a startup. Startups carry high risk because they are in early development and often lack a proven track record. If the company succeeds, the returns can be extraordinary. Early investors in companies like Uber or Airbnb saw their investments multiply many times over as these businesses became industry leaders. However, a significant percentage of startups do fail, which can mean losing your entire investment. This reality underscores the importance of understanding the **risk-reward** trade-off and being prepared for various possible outcomes.

Looking at historical data can help clarify the risk-reward profiles of different investments. Examining past performance allows individuals to identify trends and patterns that might inform future choices. For instance, the S&P 500 index has delivered an average annual return of about 7-10% over the long term. This information can help set realistic expectations, but it's essential to remember that past results don't guarantee future performance. Market conditions, economic changes, and unexpected events can all significantly impact returns.

Diversification is a key strategy for managing risk and optimizing returns, especially for those just starting their investment journey. By spreading investments across various asset classes—like equities, fixed-income securities, and real estate—you can help reduce the overall risk of your portfolio. This thoughtful approach ensures that a decline in one asset class doesn't have an outsized effect on your entire investment. For instance, if the stock market experiences a 10% drop, gains in bonds or real estate could help cushion those losses, contributing to a more stable overall value. While diversification won't eliminate risk completely, it does lessen it by avoiding heavy reliance on a single asset class.

Asset allocation is another important aspect of your investment strategy. Distributing investments among different asset classes should reflect your specific financial goals, personal risk tolerance, and investment time horizon. A well-structured allocation plan considers your unique financial situation and helps balance potential risks with expected rewards. For example, a young investor with a 30-year investment horizon might allocate:

- 80% of their portfolio to equities, which, despite their volatility, have historically provided higher long-term returns.
- A more conservative allocation for someone nearing retirement, perhaps placing 60% in bonds to preserve capital and generate steady income.

Dollar-cost averaging is a practical approach to lessen the impact of market volatility. By committing a fixed amount of capital at regular intervals—like monthly or quarterly—regardless of market conditions, you can average out the cost of your investments over time. This method allows you to buy more shares when prices are low and fewer shares when prices are high, effectively lowering your average cost per share. For instance, investing $100 each month in a mutual fund means acquiring more shares during market downturns and fewer during upswings, allowing you to benefit from market fluctuations without the stress of trying to time the market.

Setting realistic return expectations is essential for maintaining a balanced investment strategy. These expectations should be rooted in current market conditions and aligned with your personal financial objectives. While historical performance data can serve as a helpful benchmark, it's important to remember that past performance doesn't guarantee future results. For example, the S&P 500 has historically returned about 7-10% annually, but future returns may vary due to economic changes, market dynamics, and unexpected events. Aligning your return expectations with your financial goals and risk tolerance can help prevent disappointment and foster a long-term perspective.

Maintaining a balanced portfolio requires regular review and adjustment. As your financial circumstances, objectives, and risk tolerance evolve, your investment strategy should adapt accordingly. Significant life events—like a job change, marriage, or the arrival of a child—can greatly shift your financial priorities. Additionally, changes in market conditions may necessitate a reassessment of your asset allocation. Taking the time to review your portfolio at least once a year or after major life changes ensures it remains aligned with your objectives and risk profile.

Staying informed about market trends and economic indicators is vital for effective risk management and return optimization. Regularly engaging with financial news, investment newsletters, and analyses from reputable experts can provide valuable insights for your investment decisions. Many platforms offer analytical tools and resources that help track trends and evaluate economic data, equipping you with the information needed to make informed choices.

Building a successful investment strategy is an ongoing journey of learning and adaptation. As you gain experience and knowledge, you'll become more adept at navigating the complexities of the market. Connecting with investment communities, both online and in-person, can offer support and insights from seasoned individuals. These interactions can deepen your understanding and boost your confidence, empowering you to make decisions that align with your financial objectives.

Emotions play a significant role in investment decisions and can influence even the most analytical investors. **Fear** and **anxiety** often arise in response to risk, particularly during market downturns. These feelings can lead to impulsive actions like panic selling, which may lock in losses instead of allowing the market the time it needs to recover. Recognizing these emotional triggers is essential for maintaining discipline in your investment approach.

Adopting a long-term perspective can help manage emotions by keeping your focus on overall financial goals rather than reacting to short-term market fluctuations. For example, if you have a diversified portfolio and the market experiences a temporary drop, it's important to remember that history shows markets typically recover over time. By concentrating on long-term performance metrics, you can avoid making hasty decisions based on fleeting market changes.

Emotional resilience is also vital for navigating the psychological aspects of investing. Setting clear goals provides direction and purpose, making it easier to stay focused during turbulent times. Your objectives should follow the *SMART* criteria:

- specific
- measurable
- achievable
- relevant
- time-bound

For instance, instead of saying, "I want to be wealthy," consider setting a specific target like, "I aim to accumulate $50,000 for a down payment on a house within five years."

A well-defined strategy is crucial. Create a detailed plan that outlines your **asset allocation, risk tolerance**, and **investment timeline**. Sticking to this approach helps minimize the influence of emotions on your decisions. If your plan includes **dollar-cost averaging**, continue investing a fixed amount at regular intervals, regardless of market conditions. This disciplined method helps you resist the temptation to time the market, which can be challenging even for seasoned investors.

Support from investment communities or financial advisors can enhance your emotional stability. Connecting with individuals who share similar financial goals offers valuable insights and encouragement. Online forums, social media groups, and local investment clubs are excellent places to meet like-minded investors. Consulting a financial advisor can also provide personalized guidance and reassurance, especially during uncertain times.

Reflecting on your own experiences with risk and reward helps build confidence and makes you a more informed investor. Take time to review past decisions—both successes and setbacks—to identify which strategies worked and which didn't. This self-reflection uncovers behavioral patterns and empowers you to make better choices in the future. For example, if you notice a tendency to sell during downturns, you can establish rules for selling based on your investment goals rather than reacting to market fluctuations.

Tip

Feeling anxious about market ups and downs? Create a written investment plan that includes your goals, risk tolerance, and regular review dates. This roadmap helps you stay focused and avoid emotional decisions, especially when markets get volatile. Remember, sticking to your plan—even during downturns—can be your best defense against panic selling. Connect with online investment communities for support and fresh perspectives. Over time, discipline and community can help you build confidence and resilience as a new investor.

Chapter 5: Setting Clear and Achievable Financial Goals

Understanding your current financial situation is the first step toward effective planning. Begin with a personal financial assessment, which is essential for setting clear and achievable goals. Gather all relevant information, including detailed records of your income, expenses, debts, and savings. This comprehensive overview will be the foundation for your strategy.

List every source of income, such as:

- Your main salary
- Freelance work
- Additional earnings from side projects

Break down your monthly expenses into categories:

- Fixed costs like rent, mortgage payments, and utilities
- Variable expenses such as dining out, entertainment, and discretionary spending

Don't forget to include all outstanding debts, like student loans, credit card balances, and personal loans. Take a moment to assess your savings, whether they're in a traditional account, an emergency fund, or various investment accounts.

Once you have a clear picture of your finances, reflect on your personal values and how they shape your goals. Think about what matters most to you—whether it's achieving financial security, funding travel, investing in education, or supporting family members. Let these values guide your goal-setting process, ensuring your objectives feel meaningful and motivating.

Set **Specific**, **Measurable**, **Achievable**, **Relevant**, and **Time-bound** (SMART) goals to transform broad ambitions into actionable plans. For example, instead of saying, "I want to save money," define a SMART goal like, "I will save $5,000 for an emergency fund within the next 12 months by setting aside $417 each month." This approach makes your goal specific (saving $5,000), measurable (tracking monthly contributions), achievable (based on your assessment), relevant (aligned with your value of financial security), and time-bound (to be completed within 12 months). Prioritize your goals so you can focus on what matters most at different stages of life. Differentiate between short-term and long-term objectives. Short-term goals might include saving for a vacation or paying off a small debt within a year, while long-term goals could involve building retirement savings or buying a home. Ensure these objectives fit your current life stage and aspirations to keep them relevant and attainable.

Utilize tools and templates such as budgeting apps or spreadsheets to track your income, expenses, and savings. These resources provide a clear overview of your financial status. Apps like *Mint* or *YNAB* (You Need A Budget) offer user-friendly features that simplify budgeting and goal tracking.

Financial planning requires flexibility. Your objectives should adapt to changes like career shifts, unexpected expenses, or new personal circumstances. Regularly review and adjust them to stay aligned with your evolving values and available resources.

Celebrating small milestones along the way helps you stay motivated and engaged with your financial goals. Take time to acknowledge and reward yourself for reaching interim targets, such as hitting a savings milestone or paying off a debt. These celebrations reinforce positive habits and encourage you to pursue even bigger goals.

Chapter 6: Designing Your First Simple Investment Plan

A tailored investment plan serves as the cornerstone for effectively managing your financial resources. This structured guide helps you navigate the complexities of the financial world with confidence. To build a strong strategy, focus on three main components: **risk tolerance**, **investment horizon**, and **asset allocation**. Each of these elements plays a vital role in shaping a plan that aligns with your financial goals and comfort level.

Risk tolerance measures how much fluctuation in returns you are willing to accept, reflecting your readiness to handle both losses and gains. People vary widely in this regard, and that's perfectly okay! To determine your risk tolerance, consider factors such as:

- Age
- Income stability
- Financial goals
- Emotional responses to market ups and downs

A structured questionnaire can help clarify your position. Think about questions like: How would I feel if my portfolio dropped by 10% in a year? Do I want to protect my capital above all, or am I aiming for higher returns? Your answers will help categorize you as a conservative, moderate, or aggressive investor.

Investment horizon refers to how long you plan to keep your money invested before needing access. This timeline significantly influences your choices. Short-term strategies, lasting less than three years, focus on liquidity and capital protection, making them suitable for goals like paying for a vacation or a car down payment. Medium-term strategies, covering three to ten years, aim to balance growth and stability, making them a good fit for buying a home or funding education. Long-term strategies, extending beyond ten years, usually focus on growth and can handle more volatility, making them well-suited for retirement savings or wealth building.

Asset allocation means spreading investments across different asset classes—such as stocks, bonds, and cash—to balance risk and reward according to your needs. Diversification plays a key role in managing risk, as a decline in one asset class won't have an outsized effect on your entire portfolio. For those new to investing, understanding basic asset allocation models is important. These models generally fall into three types: conservative, moderate, and aggressive portfolios.

A **conservative portfolio** is best for individuals with low risk tolerance or a short investment horizon. It focuses on preserving capital and generating steady income, often by allocating a large share to bonds and cash. For example, it might include:

- 20% stocks
- 50% bonds
- 30% cash

This approach reduces volatility and provides stable income, making it a good choice for those nearing retirement or seeking minimal risk.

A **moderate portfolio** aims to strike a balance between risk and reward. It appeals to investors with medium risk tolerance and a longer investment horizon, seeking growth while maintaining some stability. A typical moderate portfolio might allocate:

- 50% stocks
- 40% bonds
- 10% cash

This mix allows for growth through equities, while bonds and cash help cushion against market downturns.

An **aggressive portfolio** suits those with high risk tolerance and a long investment horizon. The main goal is to maximize growth, so a large portion goes into stocks. An aggressive portfolio might consist of:

- 80% stocks
- 15% bonds
- 5% cash

This setup works well for younger investors or anyone with a long-term outlook, as it can weather market swings and take advantage of the higher returns that equities can offer.

Choosing suitable investment vehicles requires thoughtful analysis of each option's unique characteristics, benefits, and risks. This approach empowers you to make decisions that resonate with your financial goals and comfort with risk. Many small-scale investors find **exchange-traded funds (ETFs)**, **index funds**, and **micro-investing platforms** appealing due to their accessibility and potential for diversification.

ETFs are investment funds traded on stock exchanges, much like individual stocks. They offer a diversified portfolio of assets, which can include equities, fixed-income securities, or commodities. One of their standout features is **liquidity**; investors can buy and sell throughout the trading day at current market prices, allowing for quick responses to market shifts. Additionally, ETFs often have lower expense ratios than mutual funds, making them a budget-friendly choice for those just starting out. However, keep in mind that trading fees can add up if you frequently buy and sell shares.

Index funds, on the other hand, are mutual funds designed to replicate the performance of a specific market index, such as the S&P 500. These funds provide broad market exposure and are celebrated for their low costs and passive management style. Since they aim to match, rather than outperform, the market, index funds typically have lower fees than actively managed options. This makes them an attractive choice for those looking to minimize costs while still accessing a diverse range of assets. Unlike ETFs, index funds are priced once daily after the market closes, which means they don't offer the same intraday trading flexibility.

Micro-investing platforms like Acorns and Stash have become favorites among small-scale investors because they allow you to start with very little money. Users can invest spare change from everyday purchases into diversified portfolios. The main advantage here is **accessibility**; even a few dollars can get you started, which is perfect for newcomers. Many of these platforms also provide educational resources to help enhance your financial knowledge. However, it's wise to review fees, as they can be relatively high compared to the small amounts invested.

When comparing these options, it's important to consider:

- Fees
- Minimum investment requirements

- Liquidity

ETFs and index funds generally have lower fees than actively managed funds, but be sure to check specific expense ratios and any additional costs, such as ETF trading fees. Minimum investment amounts can vary widely; some index funds may require several thousand dollars to start, while ETFs and micro-investing platforms often have no minimums, making them more accessible for those with limited funds. Liquidity is also a key factor; ETFs provide the most flexibility with intraday trading, while index funds and micro-investing platforms may have more limitations.

Starting with low-cost, diversified funds helps new investors manage risk and gain exposure to broader markets. **Diversification** reduces the impact of poor performance in any single asset, which is especially important for beginners. Spreading investments across different asset classes and sectors can lead to more stable returns over time.

Thorough research is essential when selecting investment vehicles. Utilize reputable financial websites and analytical tools to compare and evaluate your options. Resources like *Morningstar* and *Investopedia* offer valuable information on fund performance, fees, and other key metrics. If you're seeking personalized advice, consider consulting financial professionals who can help assess your risk tolerance, set realistic goals, and create a tailored investment strategy.

Once you have clearly defined your financial goals, risk tolerance, and chosen investment vehicles, the next step is to bring these elements together into a structured plan. Start by determining a realistic initial investment amount that aligns with your current financial situation, considering your monthly income, fixed and variable expenses, and any existing savings or debts. A practical approach is to set aside a small, manageable portion of your monthly income for investments—this could be anywhere from $25 to $50, depending on what feels comfortable for you. The key is to begin with an amount that won't disrupt your financial stability but still allows you to engage with the market.

Making regular contributions to your portfolio is essential, no matter how small. These consistent investments can accumulate significantly over time, thanks to the power of **compound interest**. For instance, investing $50 each month with an average annual return of 7% could grow to more than $24,000 in 20 years. This growth comes from both ongoing contributions and the interest earned on previous gains, which helps your wealth build more quickly.

It's important to review and update your investment strategy regularly to keep it aligned with your evolving goals and circumstances. Major life events—such as starting a new job, getting married, or welcoming a child—can shift your financial priorities and risk tolerance. Changes in the market may also prompt you to rethink your asset allocation. Make it a habit to check your portfolio at least once a year or after significant life changes. During these reviews, take a moment to measure your progress toward your financial objectives and make any necessary adjustments.

To keep track of performance, take advantage of digital tools and resources. Online brokerage platforms and financial apps allow you to monitor your investments, set alerts for market changes, and access educational materials. Services like *Robinhood, E*TRADE,* and *Charles Schwab* provide user-friendly interfaces for managing your assets and staying informed about trends. Many of these platforms also offer analytical tools that help you compare your portfolio's performance to relevant benchmarks, so you can see if you're on the right path.

Keeping up with market trends and economic news is crucial for making informed choices. Check reputable financial news sources such as *The Wall Street Journal, Bloomberg,* or *CNBC* to stay updated on movements and key economic indicators. Understanding these trends can help you anticipate changes in the market and adjust your approach when needed.

Patience and discipline play a major role in sticking to your plan. Building wealth through investing takes time, consistent effort, and a willingness to learn from both successes and setbacks. Stay focused on your long-term goals and avoid reacting impulsively to short-term market swings. Emotional resilience helps you maintain discipline and prevents rash decisions driven by fear or greed.

Sticking to your investment strategy is important, but staying flexible is equally necessary. Adaptability allows you to respond to changing circumstances and seize new opportunities. For example, if a particular asset class continues to underperform, you might consider shifting your funds to more promising investments. If your financial goals change, update your approach to reflect your new priorities.

Choosing Your Ideal Starting Investment Amount

Start the process of determining the right initial investment amount with a thoughtful review of your monthly budget to identify your disposable income. This involves creating a detailed budget that separates expenses into three main categories: **essentials**, **discretionary spending**, and **savings**. Essentials include both fixed and variable costs such as rent, utilities, groceries, and transportation—necessary for maintaining daily life. Discretionary spending covers non-essential items like dining out, entertainment, and hobbies, which can be adjusted based on your financial goals. Savings should be set aside for both short-term plans, like vacations, and long-term security, such as building an emergency fund.

Begin by listing all sources of income, including your main salary, freelance work, and side projects. Next, sort your monthly expenses into the categories mentioned above. This approach provides a clear picture of your spending patterns and helps you spot areas where you can cut back to free up more money for investing. For instance, reducing discretionary spending by limiting dining out to once a week or canceling rarely used subscriptions can make more funds available for investments. Ensure your initial investment amount aligns with your **risk tolerance** and **financial security**. It's wise to keep an emergency fund that covers three to six months of living expenses to protect against unexpected costs. Once this safety net is in place, you can confidently allocate a portion of your disposable income into investments without risking your financial stability.

Set clear financial priorities to guide your investment decisions. Whether you're saving for a specific goal like a vacation or a down payment on a home, or working toward overall financial independence, these priorities will influence how much you choose to invest at the start. For example, if your main goal is to save for a down payment, you might decide to allocate a larger portion of your disposable income to investments to reach your target sooner.

Start with a small, manageable investment amount that feels comfortable for you. The regularity and frequency of your contributions matter more than the size of your first investment. Even small amounts can grow significantly over time thanks to compounding. For example, investing $25 each month with an average annual return of 7% could grow to over $12,000 in 20 years, thanks to ongoing contributions and interest earned on previous gains.

Take *Sarah's* experience as an example. She was a college student who began investing her spare change through a micro-investing app. By consistently adding small amounts, she gradually improved her financial knowledge and confidence. As her finances improved, she increased her contributions, showing how starting small can lead to substantial growth over time.

Review your investment amount regularly, especially when your income, expenses, or financial goals change. Adjust your strategy to keep it in line with your current financial priorities. For example, after a salary increase or paying off a debt, you might decide to increase your contributions.

Use budgeting apps or financial planning worksheets to track your expenses and find ways to boost your investment contributions. Tools like *Mint* or *YNAB* (You Need A Budget) offer user-friendly features for budgeting and goal tracking. These apps provide a clear overview of your finances, helping you make informed choices about your investment strategy.

Budgeting Strategies for Consistent Investing

Tip

Automate your investments by setting up an automatic transfer to your investment account each payday—even if it's just a small amount. This 'pay yourself first' approach makes investing a habit, not an afterthought. By treating your investment contribution like any other fixed expense, you'll build wealth steadily and avoid the temptation to spend what you could be investing. Start small and increase the amount as your budget allows.

To consistently allocate funds for investments, even with a limited income, a structured and disciplined budgeting strategy is essential. Begin by creating a detailed monthly budget that accurately reflects all your income sources while separating expenses into fixed and variable costs. Fixed expenses, such as **rent**, **utilities**, and **insurance**, are mandatory payments that recur each month. On the other hand, variable costs include **groceries**, **entertainment**, and **dining out**— expenses that can fluctuate and present opportunities for savings.

List all your income sources, including your primary job, freelance work, or any side gigs. This comprehensive overview will clarify your financial capacity. Next, sort your expenses. Fixed costs are typically straightforward, but variable ones may need a closer look. Track your spending for a month to identify patterns and discover areas where you can cut back. For instance, if you find yourself dining out often, preparing more meals at home can be a great way to reduce food costs.

Once you have a clear picture of your finances, seek out discretionary expenses that can be reduced or eliminated. This step is crucial for freeing up money for investments. Embrace the *pay yourself first* approach: set up an automatic transfer of a specific amount into an investment account each payday before addressing other expenses. This method helps prioritize your investing journey.

Utilizing budgeting tools like apps or spreadsheets can assist you in monitoring spending and tracking progress toward your investment goals. Applications such as **Mint** or **YNAB** (You Need A Budget) provide user-friendly interfaces that make it easier to visualize your financial status and make informed choices. Regularly review and adjust your budget to reflect any changes in income or expenses, ensuring that contributions to investments remain a priority.

Exploring ways to boost your income can further enhance your investment potential. Consider part-time work or side gigs that align with your skills and interests. Allocate a portion of this extra income to investments to accelerate your wealth accumulation. Setting specific, measurable investment goals can help maintain your motivation and commitment. Celebrate milestones along the way to reinforce your progress and keep your enthusiasm high.

Accountability can serve as a powerful motivator. Share your financial goals with a trusted friend or join a community of individuals with similar objectives for support and encouragement. These connections can offer valuable insights and help you stay on track. Using cash envelopes or digital equivalents for discretionary spending can also assist in controlling overspending and maintaining steady contributions.

Continue to learn about personal finance and investment strategies to enhance your financial literacy and make informed decisions. Explore books, online courses, and reputable financial news sources to deepen your understanding. This ongoing education will empower you to make choices that support your long-term wealth-building goals.

Chapter 7: Beginner-Friendly Digital Tools for Investors

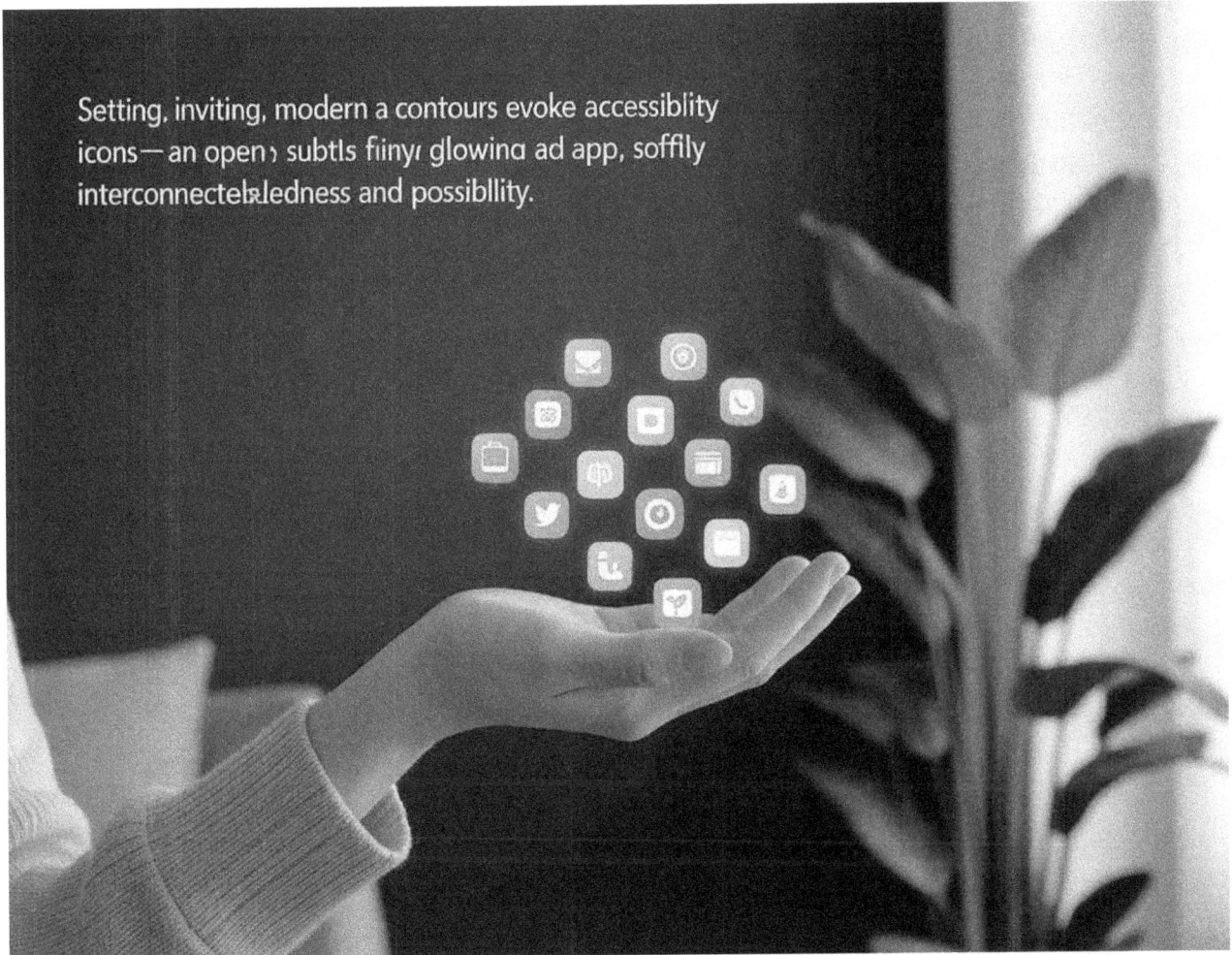

In the digital age, investing has become much more accessible, thanks to a variety of tools designed for both new and seasoned investors. These resources typically fall into four main categories:

- robo-advisors
- micro-investing apps
- brokerage platforms
- financial planning tools

Each of these serves a unique purpose and offers distinct benefits, particularly for those who are just starting their investment journey.

Robo-advisors are a great fit for beginners who prefer a more hands-off approach to investing. These platforms utilize algorithms to manage portfolios automatically, taking into account individual risk tolerance and financial goals. With lower fees compared to traditional financial advisors, robo-advisors present a budget-friendly option for those with limited funds. For example, *Betterment* offers personalized portfolio management along with features like tax-loss harvesting and automatic rebalancing, making it easier for individuals who want to steer clear of complex market analysis.

Micro-investing apps like *Acorns* empower users to invest small amounts regularly by rounding up everyday purchases to the nearest dollar and investing that spare change. This approach encourages consistent investing without the need for a hefty initial deposit. Acorns allows users to start with as little as $5, making it an inviting option for anyone who might feel daunted by traditional investment minimums. The app also provides educational materials that break down basic concepts, helping users feel more confident in their decision-making.

Brokerage platforms have become increasingly user-friendly, offering commission-free trading, a wealth of educational content, and simple interfaces that welcome newcomers. *Robinhood* exemplifies this trend, providing a platform where users can trade stocks, ETFs, and cryptocurrencies without incurring commission fees. Its clear layout and easy navigation make it appealing to new investors, and the platform includes articles and tutorials to help expand their investment knowledge.

Financial planning tools are essential for helping investors track their portfolios, set financial goals, and gain a better understanding of their overall financial situation. *Mint* shines in this category, offering features that allow users to monitor spending, create budgets, and assess performance. With a comprehensive overview of their finances, users can make informed decisions and fine-tune their strategies.

When choosing digital investment tools, security should always be a top priority. Opting for platforms with strong security measures, such as **two-factor authentication** and **data encryption**, helps protect personal and financial information from cyber threats. Many digital investment resources provide tutorials, webinars, and community forums, which are invaluable for building knowledge and confidence. Taking advantage of these resources can clarify the investment process and support users in making sound decisions.

Trying out free trials or demo accounts before committing funds allows users to become comfortable with different platforms and discover which ones align best with their goals, risk tolerance, and financial knowledge. Exploring these options helps individuals refine their strategies and set the stage for future financial growth.

Comparing Top Investment Apps for Beginners

Tip

When choosing your first investment app, focus on platforms with simple interfaces, strong customer support, and clear fee structures. Don't hesitate to use free trials or starter tiers— these let you explore features risk-free and build confidence before committing your money.

Choosing an investment app or platform can feel a bit overwhelming for beginners, especially with the multitude of options available, each showcasing its own unique features and benefits. To assist you in making a choice, this review explores several popular investment applications, emphasizing **user interface**, **accessibility**, and **customer support**—essential elements for those just starting their investment journey.

A good **user interface** is crucial in any investment app, as it significantly influences the overall experience. The best interfaces are intuitive, allowing users to easily navigate and utilize various features. Robinhood, for example, shines with its clean and simple design, making the buying and selling of stocks a breeze. Even individuals with minimal financial knowledge can quickly grasp how to make trades. Acorns also provides a user-friendly layout that supports micro-investing, enabling users to effortlessly track their investments and monitor portfolio performance.

Accessibility is another key factor. Investment platforms should function seamlessly across smartphones, tablets, and desktops to cater to different user preferences. E*TRADE and Charles Schwab, for instance, offer both mobile and desktop versions, ensuring a consistent experience whether users are at home or on the go. This flexibility allows investors to keep an eye on their portfolios and make informed decisions from anywhere. The ability to switch between devices without losing any features is particularly beneficial for those managing their investments during commutes or while traveling.

A straightforward account setup and easy navigation are vital for newcomers. Complicated or lengthy sign-up processes can deter potential investors, so platforms that provide a simple onboarding experience are highly sought after. Stash, for example, simplifies account creation by guiding users through each step with clear instructions and minimal paperwork. This approach helps alleviate the intimidation often associated with financial services, making the platform more inviting for beginners. Once an account is set up, users can quickly access educational materials, monitor their investments, and adjust their portfolios as needed, thanks to the platform's clear navigation.

Strong customer support can truly enhance the experience, especially for users who encounter issues or have questions about their investments. Access to live chat, phone support, and comprehensive FAQs offers the assistance needed to navigate the platform with confidence. Betterment, for instance, provides a robust support system that includes access to financial advisors. This ensures users can receive personalized advice when needed, which is especially valuable for beginners seeking extra guidance as they embark on their investment journey.

Educational resources are another important aspect to consider. Many investment apps offer tutorials, webinars, and community forums to help users build their financial knowledge and confidence. These tools can clarify the investment process and empower users to make informed decisions. Wealthfront, for example, provides a wealth of educational content, including articles and videos, to explain complex financial topics and support users in developing effective investment strategies.

A clear understanding of **cost structures** is essential when exploring investment apps and platforms, especially for those who are just starting their investment journey with limited capital. Each service has its own **fee model**, and these variations can significantly influence your investment returns over time. Let's take a closer look at some of the main costs you might encounter, including:

- Account maintenance fees
- Trading commissions
- Hidden charges

Account maintenance fees are quite common across many platforms. These charges may come as a flat rate or a percentage of your balance, billed either annually or monthly. For example, Betterment charges an annual fee of **0.25%** for its digital plan, which is relatively low compared to traditional financial advisors. This fee covers portfolio management and grants access to a variety of financial planning tools. If you have a larger balance, it's wise to pay attention to these costs, as they can accumulate over time and impact your long-term growth.

Trading commissions are another key consideration. Many platforms, like Robinhood, have made commission-free trading the norm, allowing users to buy and sell stocks, ETFs, and options without incurring extra charges. This approach is particularly beneficial for small-scale investors, helping them retain more of their returns by avoiding frequent trading fees. However, it's important to remain vigilant about hidden costs, such as *payment for order flow*, which can affect the price you receive when executing trades.

Some services adopt a **subscription model**, offering various tiers for a monthly or annual fee. Stash, for instance, has several subscription levels, starting at just **$1** per month for its beginner tier, which includes a personal investment account and educational resources. Higher tiers provide additional features like retirement accounts and personalized financial advice. Before selecting a subscription, it's a good idea to ensure that the included features align with your investment needs and goals.

Pay-per-use pricing models charge fees for specific actions, such as making trades or accessing premium features. This setup can be advantageous for those who trade infrequently or only require advanced tools on occasion. However, for investors who plan to be more active, these costs can add up quickly and may outweigh the benefits.

Many platforms offer free features or tiers to attract new users, which can be especially appealing for beginners looking to keep expenses low. For example, Acorns provides a free tier for college students, allowing them to access core investment services without the usual monthly fee. This enables students to start investing without incurring extra costs. Additionally, some services run promotions or offer discounts to new users, such as waiving fees for the first few months or providing bonus cash for opening an account. These offers can help ease initial expenses and make it simpler to get started.

As your portfolio grows, the long-term cost implications become increasingly important. A platform that's budget-friendly for small accounts might become more expensive as your investments increase. For instance, a low percentage-based fee could be suitable for beginners but could become costly with a larger balance. Conversely, a flat fee structure might be more cost-effective for bigger portfolios, as the fee remains constant regardless of account size.

Educational resources are essential for helping newcomers assess which investment apps and platforms suit their needs best. Many platforms understand the value of providing users with the knowledge necessary to make informed investment decisions. For instance, **Stash** offers a rich collection of articles and tutorials that simplify complex financial topics into clear, digestible pieces. This thoughtful approach helps demystify investing, making it more accessible for beginners. Similarly, **Acorns** emphasizes educational content for those new to investing, guiding users in grasping fundamental principles and understanding the potential outcomes of their financial choices.

Community support is just as vital. Platforms that cultivate a strong sense of community can significantly enhance the experience for new investors. These supportive environments allow users to share experiences, ask questions, and learn from one another. **Robinhood**, for example, boasts an active online community where individuals discuss strategies, exchange insights, and uplift each other. This kind of peer interaction is particularly beneficial for beginners who may feel isolated or overwhelmed by the complexities of investing. Being part of a community can boost confidence and provide reassurance that others are navigating similar challenges.

Customization options are important for aligning investment strategies with personal goals and risk tolerance. **Betterment** enables users to adjust their portfolios to meet specific objectives, such as saving for retirement or building an emergency fund. This level of personalization helps ensure that investment decisions reflect individual goals and comfort with risk. **Wealthfront** also provides robust customization, allowing users to modify their asset allocation and experiment with different strategies. Such flexibility is advantageous for those still exploring their financial goals and risk preferences.

Step-by-step guides and investment tutorials are particularly beneficial for those just starting out. These resources present a clear, organized way to learn about investing. **E*TRADE**, for instance, offers a variety of tutorials and webinars that cover everything from the basics of stock trading to more advanced strategies. These tools empower users to build a solid foundation of knowledge, make informed choices, and develop effective investment plans.

User communities and forums are also worth highlighting. These spaces provide new investors with opportunities to connect, share experiences, and seek advice. The *Bogleheads* community stands out as a respected forum where investors discuss strategies, offer insights, and support one another. Engaging in such communities can yield valuable information and help newcomers feel more confident in their decisions.

Portfolio management tools and the level of customization available can significantly shape a beginner's experience as well. **Charles Schwab**, for example, offers a variety of features that allow users to tailor their investments to their goals and risk tolerance. These include:

- Options for adjusting asset allocation
- Exploring different strategies
- Setting clear financial objectives

Such tools help ensure that investments align with personal needs and preferences, leading to a more tailored and effective experience.

Chapter 8: Investment Options Starting at $5

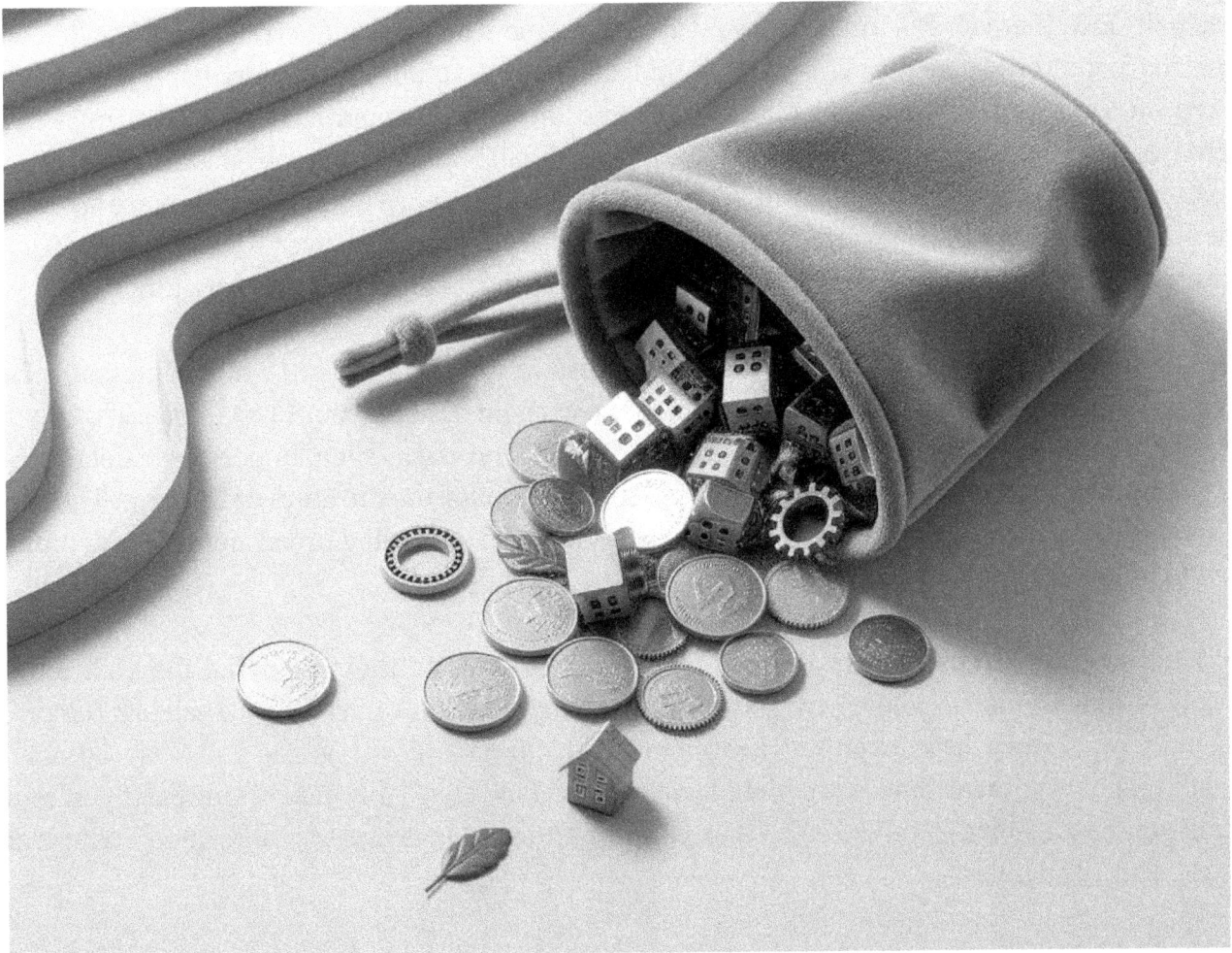

Investing with as little as $5 might seem unlikely, but thanks to modern financial tools, it's now both possible and practical. This text explores a variety of investment options tailored for small-scale investors, each offering unique features, benefits, and potential drawbacks.

Fractional shares have transformed the landscape for those eager to buy high-value stocks without needing a large sum of money. This approach allows you to own a portion of a share, making it feasible to invest in companies like *Amazon* or *Google* with just a small amount. The main advantage here is diversification, as you can spread your limited funds across several stocks, helping to reduce risk. Just be mindful of transaction fees, which can nibble away at your returns, and remember that fractional shares often come with limited or no voting rights at shareholder meetings. Beginners might find it helpful to start with a few well-researched companies and gradually expand their portfolios as they gain experience and confidence.

Exchange-traded funds (ETFs) provide another straightforward way to dip your toes into investing. These funds pool money from many investors to buy a diversified mix of stocks, bonds, or other assets, trading on stock exchanges just like individual stocks. With ETFs, even a small investment can give you access to entire markets or specific sectors, such as technology or healthcare. They offer diversification and typically have lower expense ratios than mutual funds. However, keep in mind that ETFs are still subject to market volatility, and while management fees are usually low, they can still impact your returns. Beginners might want to consider those that track broad market indices, like the *S&P 500*, to build a solid investment foundation.

Micro-savings apps like *Acorns* make saving and investing automatic by rounding up everyday purchases to the nearest dollar and investing the spare change. This approach encourages consistent investing without requiring a hefty initial deposit. The convenience and automation are significant benefits, but it's wise to be aware of service fees that can accumulate over time. To maximize the advantages of these apps, check your settings regularly and ensure the fees align with your investment goals.

Peer-to-peer lending platforms connect investors with individuals or small businesses in need of loans. By providing funds for these loans, you can earn interest on your investment. This method can offer attractive returns, but it's important to weigh the risks, such as borrower defaults and limited liquidity, which means your money could be tied up for the duration of the loan. Those new to this area should consider starting with small amounts and spreading investments across multiple loans to help lower risk.

Cryptocurrency investments have gained popularity due to their potential for high returns. Platforms like *Coinbase* allow you to start investing in digital currencies such as *Bitcoin* or *Ethereum* with very little capital. The opportunity for significant gains and easy access are appealing, but cryptocurrencies are highly volatile and face regulatory uncertainties. If you're new to this market, it's best to invest only what you can afford to lose and stay informed about trends and regulatory changes.

When considering these options, focus on building a balanced portfolio by:

- Spreading investments to manage risk
- Checking performance regularly
- Increasing amounts as your knowledge and confidence grow

Taking these steps helps you lay a strong foundation for your financial future, even if you start with limited funds.

Chapter 9: Opening Your First Investment Account

Tip

Before opening your first investment account, take advantage of demo accounts or trial periods offered by many platforms. This lets you explore features, test the interface, and build confidence—without risking any money. It's a smart way to learn the ropes and see if the platform fits your needs. Don't rush this step; a little practice now can help you avoid costly mistakes later and make your first real investment experience much smoother.

Opening your first investment account is a significant step in managing your financial portfolio. While the process may feel a bit daunting at first, clarifying your financial objectives and seeking the right guidance can make it much more approachable and empowering. Your first key decision is to select the type of account that best aligns with your investment goals. This choice will influence the assets you can invest in and the tax implications you'll encounter.

If you're looking to actively trade stocks, exchange-traded funds (ETFs), or other securities, a **brokerage account** is likely your best option. These accounts provide:

- Flexibility
- Access to a diverse range of investment products
- Real-time trading
- Various order types

On the other hand, if your primary aim is to save for retirement over the long haul, an **Individual Retirement Account (IRA)** may be more suitable. IRAs offer valuable tax benefits, such as *tax-deferred growth* or *tax-free withdrawals*, which can significantly enhance your savings over time. For those interested in digital currencies, a specialized **cryptocurrency account** allows you to trade assets like Bitcoin or Ethereum.

Once you've chosen the right account type, gather the necessary documents to ensure a smooth account opening process. You'll need:

- A government-issued ID, such as a driver's license or passport, to verify your identity.
- A Social Security number or tax identification number for tax reporting.
- Proof of address, like a recent utility bill or bank statement, to confirm your residency.

Having these documents ready in advance helps streamline the process and prevents unnecessary delays.

Each account type has its own requirements and restrictions, so it's essential to understand what's expected before opening one. Minimum deposit amounts can vary; some accounts allow you to start with as little as $0, while others may require a higher initial deposit. Be sure these requirements align with your financial situation. Account maintenance fees also differ from one platform to another, and these costs can affect your investment returns. Some platforms waive fees or reduce them if you maintain a certain balance, so it's worth exploring these options.

New investors often have concerns about privacy and data security. Addressing these worries is crucial for feeling confident about your investments. Reputable financial institutions implement robust security measures to safeguard your personal and financial information, including:

- Advanced encryption
- Two-factor authentication
- Regular security audits

When selecting a platform, look for those regulated by financial authorities to ensure they adhere to industry standards for data protection. Reviewing the institution's privacy policy will also help you understand how your data is used and protected.

Choosing a financial institution or platform is an important step that deserves thoughtful consideration to ensure it aligns with your investment preferences and goals. This choice can greatly influence your experience and financial outcomes, so taking the time to evaluate your options is essential. Let's explore the main types of platforms: **online brokers**, **robo-advisors**, and **traditional financial institutions**, each offering unique advantages and challenges.

For those who enjoy taking an active role in managing their investments, **online brokers** are often a popular choice. These platforms provide direct access to a diverse array of products, including individual stocks, exchange-traded funds (ETFs), options, and mutual funds. The primary benefit is the flexibility and control they offer, allowing you to execute trades in real time and tailor your strategy to your needs. However, this level of control does require a solid understanding of financial markets and investment principles, which can feel overwhelming for beginners. While many online brokers promote commission-free trading, it's wise to closely examine other potential costs, such as:

- account maintenance fees
- withdrawal charges
- fees for advanced trading tools

Robo-advisors are a great fit for those who prefer a more automated investment experience. These platforms utilize algorithms to create and manage a diversified portfolio based on your risk tolerance and financial objectives. Their user-friendly nature and lower management fees compared to traditional advisors make them appealing, especially for newcomers or those who favor a hands-off approach. On the flip side, this means less control over specific investment choices, and the automated setup may not be ideal for individuals seeking a more personalized strategy.

Traditional institutions like banks and credit unions also offer investment services alongside their other financial products. Their established reputations and regulatory oversight often foster a sense of security and trust. These entities may provide personalized financial advice and a wide range of services, including:

- retirement planning
- estate planning
- wealth management

However, it's important to note that fees at traditional institutions can be significantly higher, and the selection of investment options may be more limited compared to what online platforms offer.

When comparing these options, consider factors such as user interface design, customer service quality, educational resources, and fee structures. A platform with an intuitive interface is particularly important for newcomers, so look for easy navigation and clear instructions that simplify executing trades and monitoring your portfolio. Reliable customer service is also vital, especially when you encounter technical issues or have questions about your investments. Check if the platform provides multiple support channels, such as:

- live chat
- phone support
- email

Access to educational resources can greatly enhance your investment knowledge. Platforms that offer tutorials, webinars, and informative articles can support your learning journey and boost your confidence. These materials are especially beneficial for beginners, providing guidance on various strategies and current market trends. Fee structures can vary widely between platforms, so it's crucial to understand all associated costs. Look for transparent pricing and be mindful of hidden fees that could impact your returns.

Many platforms allow you to explore their features through trial periods or demo accounts, giving you the opportunity to test functionality without any financial risk. This hands-on experience can help you determine if the platform meets your investment needs.

User reviews and recommendations from trusted sources can provide valuable insights. Seek feedback from individuals with similar investment goals and experiences, as their perspectives can help you assess the platform's reliability and performance.

After selecting your platform and gathering the necessary documents, head over to the website or download the mobile app to begin setting up your account. Most services will guide you through the application process with helpful prompts, starting with creating a username and password. It's a good idea to choose a **strong password** that mixes uppercase and lowercase letters, numbers, and special characters for enhanced security. Many platforms also ask you to set up **security questions** for an extra layer of protection.

Next, you'll need to enter some personal information, including your full name, date of birth, and Social Security number. This information is essential for verifying your identity and meeting tax reporting requirements. Take a moment to double-check your entries to help avoid any delays in approval. You may also need to upload a government-issued ID and proof of address, like a recent utility bill or bank statement.

Once you've provided your details, it's time to select the type of account you'd like to open. Common options include:

- Individual brokerage accounts
- Retirement accounts like IRAs
- Specialized accounts for cryptocurrency trading

Think about your financial goals and the tax implications before making your choice. If the platform allows it, you can also name beneficiaries to ensure your assets are distributed according to your wishes.

When choosing your account type, you can opt to receive electronic statements and notifications. This choice not only helps reduce paper waste but also gives you quicker access to your account information. Updates and alerts will be sent directly to your email or mobile device, keeping you in the loop about account activity and market changes.

With your account set up, the next step is to fund it. Most platforms provide several ways to deposit money, such as:

- Bank transfers
- Wire transfers
- Check deposits

Bank transfers are typically the easiest and most cost-effective option. To initiate a transfer, link your bank account by providing your bank's routing number and your account number. Keep in mind that the verification process can take a few days, so it's good to plan for this timing. Wire transfers are faster but may come with fees, while check deposits often take longer to process.

You might experience a bit of waiting time before your funds become available, as many platforms require several business days to clear your deposit. This standard security step helps ensure the legitimacy of your funds.

Protecting your investments is important, so consider setting up **two-factor authentication (2FA)** to secure your account. This feature requires you to confirm your identity with a second method, such as a text message or authentication app, in addition to your password. Activating 2FA significantly reduces the risk of unauthorized access.

Now is a great time to explore the educational tools and resources available to you. Many platforms offer tutorials, webinars, and articles to help you grasp investment concepts and strategies. Taking advantage of these resources will enhance your financial knowledge and confidence, empowering you to make informed decisions. You can also join online forums or communities to connect with other investors, share experiences, and gather useful tips.

Chapter 10: Step-by-Step Guide to Your First Investment

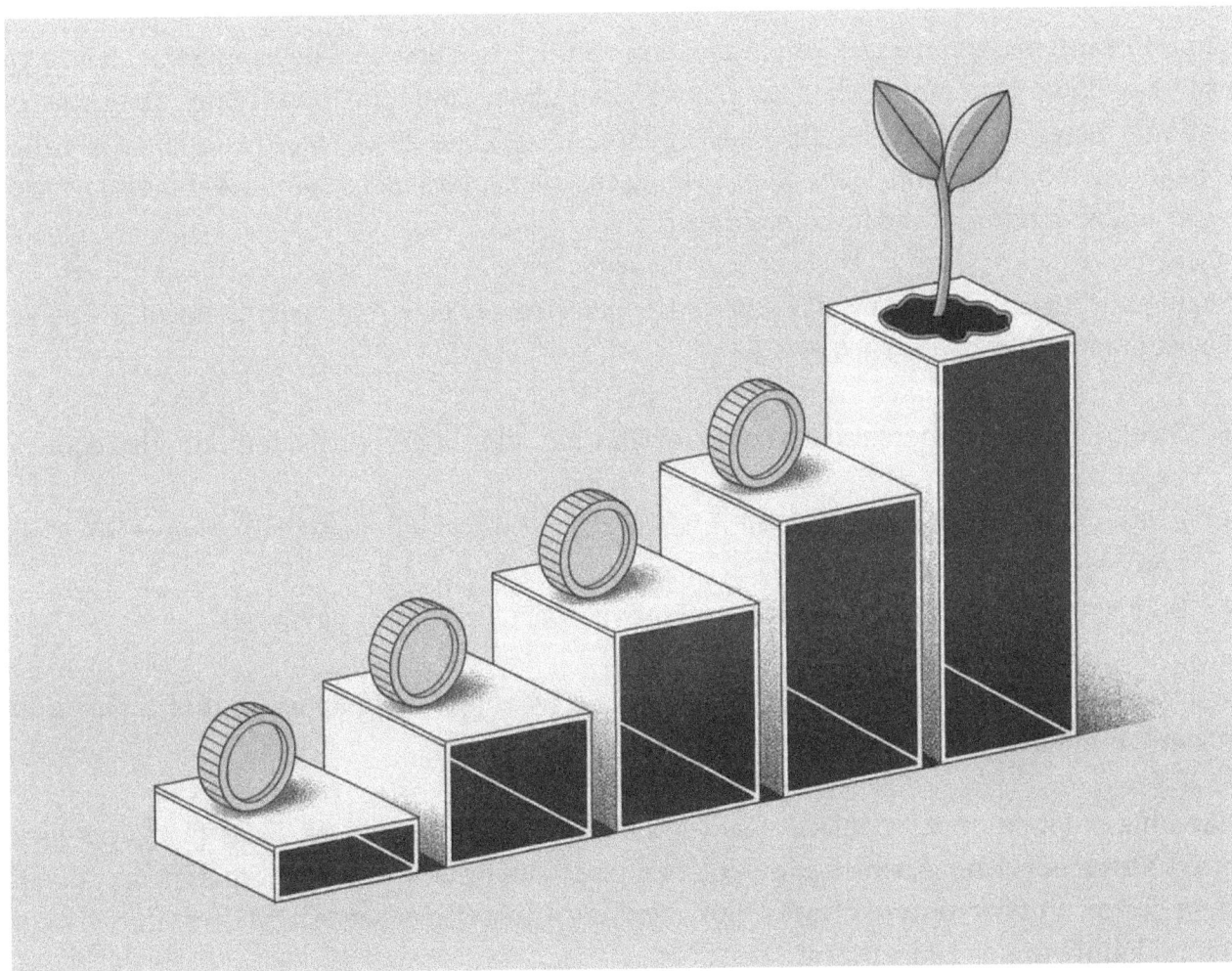

How-To

Ready to make your first investment? Start by exploring your platform's dashboard and educational resources. Use stock screeners and performance charts to research assets. Add interesting options to your watchlist. When you're confident, place a market, limit, or stop order—double-checking all details before submitting. Track your results and document your decisions to learn and grow.

Start investing by familiarizing yourself with the interface of your chosen platform, whether it's a web-based service or a mobile app. This control center is where you'll make decisions that can positively influence your financial future. Take some time to explore the dashboard, which provides a clear overview of your investments and the broader market landscape. The **portfolio overview** section is particularly important, as it displays your current holdings, their performance, and how your assets are allocated. This information is essential for tracking your progress and making informed decisions about where to invest next.

The **market news** section keeps you in the loop on the latest financial developments, helping you identify trends and economic changes that might impact your portfolio. Many platforms offer educational materials like articles, tutorials, and webinars. These resources are designed to enhance your financial knowledge and confidence, making complex topics more approachable and providing a deeper understanding of the investment world.

To begin your investing journey, navigate to the investment section of your platform. Here, you'll find a list of available assets, such as:

- Stocks: Provide ownership in a company and can offer high returns, but they also come with higher risk.
- ETFs and mutual funds: Allow for diversification by pooling money from many investors to purchase a mix of assets.
- Bonds: Generally considered safer and provide regular interest payments.

Take the time to explore each category to understand what sets them apart, as this understanding is crucial for building a well-rounded portfolio.

Researching potential investments is vital for making thoughtful choices. Most platforms include tools like **stock screeners**, which allow you to filter stocks by criteria such as market cap, dividend yield, or sector. **Performance charts** illustrate how an asset has performed over time, making it easier to identify trends and patterns.

Company profiles provide detailed information about a company's financial health, leadership, and business model. Reviewing these profiles helps you weigh the risks and rewards of investing in a particular company. When examining past performance, pay attention to metrics like the **price-to-earnings ratio**, **dividend history**, and **earnings growth rate**. These figures can give you insight into a company's value and its potential for future growth.

Assessing risk levels and possible returns is essential for making informed investment choices. Risk refers to the chance of losing money, while potential returns are the profits you might earn. Finding the right balance between these two is key to building a portfolio that aligns with your goals and comfort with risk. Use the **risk-reward formula** to help evaluate your options:

Expected Return = Risk-Free Rate + Risk Premium

This formula illustrates the extra return you might expect for taking on more risk. A higher risk premium indicates greater possible rewards, but it also entails more risk.

Before selecting an investment, consider a checklist of factors that could influence your decision. Market trends can affect how different asset classes perform. Economic indicators like interest rates, inflation, and employment statistics reveal the overall health of the economy and can impact your returns. Your personal financial goals are important too, as they guide your investment strategy and help you stay focused. Whether you're saving for a house, planning for retirement, or building an emergency fund, your goals should shape your investment choices.

After identifying a potential investment, add it to your watchlist. This step allows you to keep an eye on the asset's performance over time and offers valuable insights into its price movements and market trends. To do this, simply navigate to the asset's page on your platform and look for the option labeled "**Add to Watchlist**" or something similar. Tracking an asset in this way enables you to observe its behavior under various market conditions without committing any funds.

When you're ready to make your first investment, choose the type of order you want to place. There are three main types:

- Market orders: Instruct your broker to buy or sell an asset immediately at the best available price. This is effective when you want to execute a trade quickly and aren't too concerned about the exact price. Just keep in mind that the final execution price might differ slightly from the last quoted price due to real-time market changes.

- Limit orders: Allow you to set the maximum price you're willing to pay when buying or the minimum price you'll accept when selling. This is particularly useful if you have a specific price target and are willing to wait for the market to reach it. For instance, if a stock is trading at $50 and you want to buy at $48, you can set a limit order at that price. The order will only go through if the stock's price drops to $48 or lower.

- Stop orders: Also known as stop-loss orders, help limit potential losses by triggering a market order once the asset hits a certain price. For example, if you own a stock valued at $60 and want to guard against a significant drop, you can set a stop order at $55. If the price falls to that level, the stop order turns into a market order and sells the stock at the best available price.

To place an order, head to the trading section of your platform and select the asset you want to trade. Enter the order details, including the type, quantity, and any price limits or stop prices. Choose a time-in-force option, which determines how long the order stays active. Common choices are:

- Day: The order expires at the end of the trading day if not executed.
- Good 'Til Canceled: The order remains active until you cancel it or it's executed.

Before submitting your order, take a moment to check all the details. Ensure the order type, quantity, and price limits align with your investment strategy. Reviewing these details helps prevent mistakes and ensures your trade goes through as planned.

After placing your order, keep an eye on your investment. Utilize portfolio tracking tools to see how your assets are performing and make adjustments if needed. These tools provide insights into your portfolio's overall value, how each asset is doing, and any market changes that could affect your investments.

It's also a good idea to keep a record of your investment decisions. Document the reasons for each trade, the results, and any lessons learned. This practice helps you refine your strategy over time, building on successes and learning from setbacks.

Chapter 11: Growing Your Portfolio with Patience

Tip

Automating your investments—through systematic investment plans or dividend reinvestment—removes the guesswork and emotional stress from building wealth. By setting up automatic contributions and reinvesting earnings, you create a steady, disciplined approach that works quietly in the background. This not only helps you stay consistent but also takes advantage of compounding, making your money work harder for you over time.

Consistency and discipline are key ingredients for achieving meaningful portfolio growth, especially when starting with limited financial resources. Creating a **systematic investment plan** (SIP) or setting up automatic contributions can significantly enhance your investment journey. These strategies simplify the process and help cultivate a habit of regular investing, which is vital for building wealth over time.

A systematic investment plan involves committing to invest a set amount of money at regular intervals, such as monthly or quarterly. This approach is particularly beneficial for new investors, as it minimizes the emotional decision-making that often comes with market fluctuations. By automating contributions, you make investing a regular part of your financial routine, much like paying monthly bills or saving for a special trip. This consistency not only supports gradual wealth accumulation but also eases the stress of trying to time the market.

Dollar-cost averaging is one of the standout features of a SIP. This strategy entails investing a fixed amount of money into a specific investment, like a stock or mutual fund, at regular intervals, regardless of the asset's current price. The primary benefit is its ability to soften the impact of market ups and downs on your investments. When prices are high, your fixed investment buys fewer shares; when prices drop, you acquire more. Over time, this method can lower the average cost per share and may enhance overall returns.

Imagine investing $100 each month in a mutual fund. In a fluctuating market, the price of the fund can vary quite a bit. For instance, if the price per share is $10 one month, you would buy 10 shares. If the price falls to $8 the next month, you could purchase 12.5 shares. Over time, this approach can lead to a lower average cost per share compared to making a single lump-sum investment.

Historical data showcases the effectiveness of this strategy. Investing $100 monthly in the *S&P 500* index over the past 30 years would have exposed you to a variety of market conditions, including downturns and bull markets. Despite these fluctuations, consistent investing would have resulted in significant growth, thanks to the compounding effect and the market's long-term upward trend.

Compounding plays a powerful role in your investment strategy. This process allows the returns on investments to generate additional returns. Even modest, regular contributions can accumulate into a substantial sum over time. For example, starting with $1,000 and adding $100 each month at an average annual return of 7% could grow your investment to over $120,000 in 30 years. This growth stems from both your contributions and the interest earned on previous gains, which accelerates your financial progress.

Setting realistic financial goals and timelines is essential for aligning your investment strategy with your personal financial situation and risk tolerance. Start by evaluating your current financial status, including income, expenses, and any outstanding debts. This assessment will help you determine how much you can comfortably invest each month without compromising your financial stability.

Clearly define your objectives. Are you saving for a down payment on a home, preparing for retirement, or building an emergency fund? Each goal requires a different timeline and risk profile. For instance, saving for a short-term goal like a vacation may call for a more conservative investment strategy, while investing for retirement, which could be decades away, might justify taking on higher risks for potentially greater returns.

Matching contributions to your risk tolerance is crucial. This reflects your ability and willingness to handle market fluctuations, which can vary from person to person based on factors like age, income, and financial goals. A younger investor with a stable income and a long investment horizon may feel comfortable with a higher-risk portfolio, while someone nearing retirement might prefer a more conservative approach.

Establishing realistic goals and aligning your investment strategy with your risk tolerance creates a structured plan for your financial objectives. This plan guides your investment decisions and helps maintain focus and motivation, even during market downturns. Remember, successful investing relies less on trying to time the market and more on staying invested for the long haul. Consistency, discipline, and a long-term perspective are your most valuable allies in building wealth over time.

Diversification is a fundamental aspect of a robust investment strategy, helping to reduce risk while fostering portfolio growth. By spreading investments across various asset classes, sectors, and geographic regions, you can significantly minimize the impact of any single investment's poor performance on your overall portfolio. This thoughtful approach not only manages risk but also opens up exciting opportunities for growth across different markets and economic conditions.

To diversify effectively, it's essential to familiarize yourself with the main asset classes available, which typically include:

- Equities (stocks)
- Fixed income (bonds)
- Real estate
- Commodities

Each class responds differently to changing market conditions, providing a buffer against volatility. For example, while equities can offer high returns, they also come with higher risk. In contrast, fixed income securities tend to provide more stability and steady income, helping to balance the fluctuations of stocks.

Sector diversification is another important piece of the puzzle. Within the equity market, sectors like *technology, healthcare, finance,* and *consumer goods* each react uniquely to economic cycles and industry trends. By spreading investments across multiple sectors, you can reduce the risks associated with downturns in any one industry. If the technology sector faces challenges, gains in healthcare could help offset those losses, keeping your portfolio on a steady course.

Geographic diversification involves placing investments in different countries and regions, which helps reduce exposure to economic or political issues in any single nation. For instance, if the U.S. market is experiencing difficulties, markets in Asia or Europe might be thriving, providing a safeguard for your investments. **Exchange-traded funds (ETFs)** and **mutual funds** focused on international markets are practical tools to achieve this kind of diversification.

When selecting a mix of assets, it's important to consider how they interact with one another. **Correlation** measures this relationship, and including assets with low or negative correlations can help smooth out your portfolio's overall performance. Many financial platforms offer correlation matrices to assist in analyzing these connections, empowering you to make informed investment choices.

Maintaining a diversified portfolio requires regular rebalancing. Over time, the value of different assets will change, which can disrupt your original allocation. For example, if stocks perform particularly well, they may occupy a larger share of your portfolio than intended, increasing your risk. Rebalancing involves periodically reviewing and adjusting your asset mix to ensure it aligns with your goals and risk tolerance.

To rebalance, start by checking your current asset allocation against your target. If you notice discrepancies, consider:

- Selling some of the assets that have grown too large
- Buying more of those that are underrepresented

This approach helps keep your risk level in check and encourages disciplined investing, as it often involves selling assets that have performed well and purchasing those that haven't.

Reinvesting dividends and interest is a fantastic strategy to enhance the growth rate of your investment portfolio. When you choose to put these earnings back into your investments, your capital begins to generate additional returns, amplifying the compounding effect that fuels exponential growth over time. **Compounding** means that the returns from your investments start earning their own returns, creating a snowball effect that can lead to significant wealth accumulation.

Consider the impact of reinvesting dividends. Imagine you own 100 shares of a company that pays an annual dividend of $2 per share, providing you with $200 in income each year. If you decide to reinvest these dividends instead of withdrawing them, you can use the $200 to purchase more shares of the company. Over time, these new shares will also pay dividends, which you can reinvest to acquire even more shares. This ongoing process increases your total number of shares, resulting in a larger dividend payout each year.

The compounding principle applies similarly to interest earned from bonds or savings accounts. By reinvesting the interest, you increase your principal, which then earns more interest in the future. The **compound interest formula** beautifully captures this effect:

$$A = P \left(1 + \frac{r}{n}\right)^{nt}$$

In this formula, A represents the total amount accumulated after n years, including interest, P is the initial principal, r is the annual interest rate, and t is the investment period in years. Reinvesting dividends and interest boosts the principal P, leading to greater growth over time.

Setting up automatic reinvestment through your brokerage account makes it simple to take advantage of this strategy. Most online brokerages offer a **Dividend Reinvestment Plan (DRIP)**, which automatically uses your dividends to buy more shares of the same stock. To activate this feature, just head to your account settings and select the reinvest dividends option. This ensures your earnings are consistently reinvested, eliminating the need for manual transactions and supporting a disciplined approach to long-term growth.

Reinvesting dividends and interest over the long term can truly make a difference. For example, an investor who puts $10,000 into a stock with a 3% annual dividend yield and reinvests the dividends, while the stock grows at an average annual rate of 5%, could see the investment grow to over $43,000 in 30 years. In contrast, if the dividends are not reinvested, the same investment would reach only about $34,000. This example illustrates how reinvesting can significantly enhance your portfolio's value over time.

Tracking your reinvestment progress is a great way to measure its impact on your portfolio's performance. Many brokerage platforms offer tools and reports that allow you to monitor the number of shares you own, the dividends you've received, and your total investment value. Regularly reviewing this information helps you see how reinvesting contributes to your wealth and empowers you to make informed decisions about your investment strategy.

Investing requires both financial expertise and a solid psychological foundation, as the emotional challenges can feel particularly daunting for those just starting out. Traits like **patience** and **emotional resilience** are essential, helping you stick to your investment plan during turbulent times and avoid missteps that could sidetrack your financial aspirations.

One significant emotional hurdle for investors is the urge to react to market fluctuations. When markets dip, many feel the pressure to sell off investments to prevent further losses. Acting on this impulse often results in locking in losses instead of giving your investments a chance to bounce back. Remember, market ups and downs are a normal part of investing, and history shows that they typically recover over time. Keeping a long-term perspective can help you steer clear of hasty decisions driven by short-term movements.

Chasing quick profits is another common trap. The allure of fast gains can lead to frequent buying and selling in hopes of capitalizing on trends, but this strategy often results in higher transaction costs and poorly timed trades. By focusing on building a diversified portfolio that aligns with your long-term goals, you can resist the temptation to chase fleeting opportunities, manage risk effectively, and enhance your returns over time.

To cultivate a long-term investment mindset, consider strategies that encourage patience and alleviate anxiety. You might find the following practices helpful:

- Set regular times to review your portfolio, such as quarterly or semi-annually, to stay informed without getting overwhelmed by daily fluctuations.
- Use these scheduled assessments to evaluate performance and make necessary adjustments while maintaining a broader outlook.
- Focus on your long-term objectives rather than getting distracted by short-term noise.

Checking your portfolio less frequently is another effective way to nurture patience. Constant monitoring can heighten stress and make it more challenging to resist impulsive reactions to market changes. Trust the investment plan you've crafted and give it time to work, as achieving meaningful results requires long-term commitment and perseverance.

Staying informed about market trends and economic indicators is important for making sound decisions, but it's equally vital to maintain perspective and not let this information dictate your every move. Use market data to guide your approach, but always keep your long-term goals at the forefront. This mindset helps you remain adaptable and resilient, even when conditions are unpredictable.

Emotional resilience is crucial for navigating the psychological aspects of investing. Establishing clear investment rules and consistently following them can help minimize the impact of emotions on your decisions. For instance, if your plan includes *dollar-cost averaging*, continue investing a set amount at regular intervals, regardless of market conditions. This disciplined approach helps you avoid the temptation to time the market, a challenge that even seasoned investors encounter.

Engaging with investment communities or seeking advice from financial professionals can bolster your emotional stability. Connecting with others who share similar financial goals provides valuable support and insights. Online forums, social media groups, and local investment clubs offer opportunities to network with like-minded individuals. Additionally, seeking guidance from a financial advisor can provide personalized advice and reassurance, especially during uncertain times.

Consistency and Dollar-Cost Averaging for Steady Wealth

Tip

Automate your investments to stay consistent, even when life gets busy or markets get rocky. Setting up automatic transfers means you won't have to rely on willpower or perfect timing— your money keeps working for you, rain or shine. This simple step helps you build wealth steadily, reduces the temptation to skip contributions, and makes investing feel effortless. Start small, stay regular, and let automation do the heavy lifting.

Consistency in investing is much like the nurturing care required in gardening. Just as a tree needs regular watering and thoughtful nutrient management to grow strong and bear fruit, an investment portfolio flourishes when you make consistent contributions. This approach emphasizes the importance of smaller, regular investments rather than attempting to time the market or making large, sporadic transactions. By adhering to this disciplined method, you can harness the power of **compounding growth**, where returns begin to generate additional earnings over time, ultimately leading to significant wealth accumulation.

Consider the process of planting a seed. Initially, it may seem small and unremarkable, but with steady care, it can develop into a thriving tree. In the same way, small, regular investments can accumulate into substantial wealth over the years. The key is to keep contributing, much like ensuring your tree receives enough water and sunlight. This consistency allows you to benefit from compounding, as investment returns start to generate their own returns, creating an exponential growth effect that accelerates your financial journey.

To cultivate a consistent investment habit, begin with a few practical steps:

- Select specific dates for your contributions—whether monthly or bi-weekly, depending on your financial situation.
- Align your investment schedule with your pay cycle to make this process a seamless part of your routine.
- Set up automatic transfers from your bank account to your investment platform. Automation ensures that contributions occur on schedule, minimizing the risk of manual errors or skipping a contribution due to market fluctuations or personal financial pressures.

Maintaining consistency can sometimes be a challenge. Financial disruptions, such as unexpected expenses or changes in income, may disrupt your routine. Market downturns can also tempt you to pause contributions during uncertain times. To navigate these challenges, keep a long-term perspective and understand that market fluctuations are a normal aspect of investing. Historical data shows that markets generally recover over time. By focusing on your long-term financial goals, you can avoid reacting impulsively to short-term market movements.

Having a well-funded **emergency fund** can provide a financial safety net, allowing you to continue your contributions even during difficult times. This fund can cover unexpected expenses without forcing you to alter your strategy. Regularly reviewing your budget can also help identify areas where you can cut back, freeing up more resources for investments.

Setting realistic investment goals is another effective way to maintain consistency. Clear, achievable objectives keep you motivated and focused on your long-term plans. These goals should be specific and measurable, such as saving a certain amount for a home down payment or building a retirement fund. Tracking your progress toward these goals allows you to celebrate small milestones, reinforcing your commitment to regular investing.

Dollar-cost averaging (DCA) is a thoughtful investment strategy that can be especially beneficial for those just starting their journey to build wealth over time. By committing a fixed dollar amount to investments at regular intervals—whether weekly, monthly, or quarterly—regardless of the asset's current price, you can help soften the impact of market volatility and minimize the effects of price fluctuations. This approach allows you to purchase more shares when prices are low and fewer shares when prices are high, effectively lowering your average cost per share throughout your investment journey.

To illustrate how this strategy works, let's consider a specific scenario. Imagine you decide to invest $100 each month in a mutual fund. During a bull market, where prices are on the rise, your $100 will buy fewer shares each month as the price per share increases. Conversely, in a bear market, when prices are declining, your $100 will allow you to purchase more shares as the price drops. Over time, this method can lead to a lower average purchase price compared to making a single lump-sum investment, as it takes advantage of the natural ups and downs in market prices.

Let's take a closer look at a detailed example. Suppose you start investing in a mutual fund with monthly share prices of $10, $8, $12, $9, and $11. With DCA, your $100 monthly investment would buy:

- 10 shares in the first month
- 12.5 shares in the second month
- 8.33 shares in the third month
- 11.11 shares in the fourth month
- 9.09 shares in the fifth month

After five months, you will have invested $500 and accumulated about 51 shares, resulting in an average cost of roughly $9.80 per share. This average is lower than the highest price paid during the period, showcasing how DCA can effectively help reduce the average purchase cost.

Empirical data supports the effectiveness of this strategy for building wealth over time. For example, investing $100 monthly in the *S&P 500* index over the past 30 years would have exposed you to a variety of market conditions, including downturns and bull markets. Despite these fluctuations, consistently applying DCA would have led to significant growth, thanks to the compounding effect and the market's long-term upward trend. This historical perspective can provide reassurance to novice investors about DCA's potential to support steady wealth accumulation.

To incorporate DCA into your investment strategy, choose a fixed contribution amount and schedule that align with your financial goals and risk tolerance. Start by evaluating your current financial situation—consider your income, expenses, and any existing debts—to determine a monthly investment amount that feels comfortable and won't create financial stress. This thoughtful approach helps you maintain consistent contributions, even during challenging economic times.

Once you have set your contribution amount, establish automatic transfers from your bank account to your investment platform. Automating these contributions ensures they happen on schedule and reduces the risk of missing a payment due to market swings or personal financial issues. This routine reinforces your commitment to your investment plan, even when emotions might tempt you to make changes.

Chapter 12: Common Mistakes New Investors Make

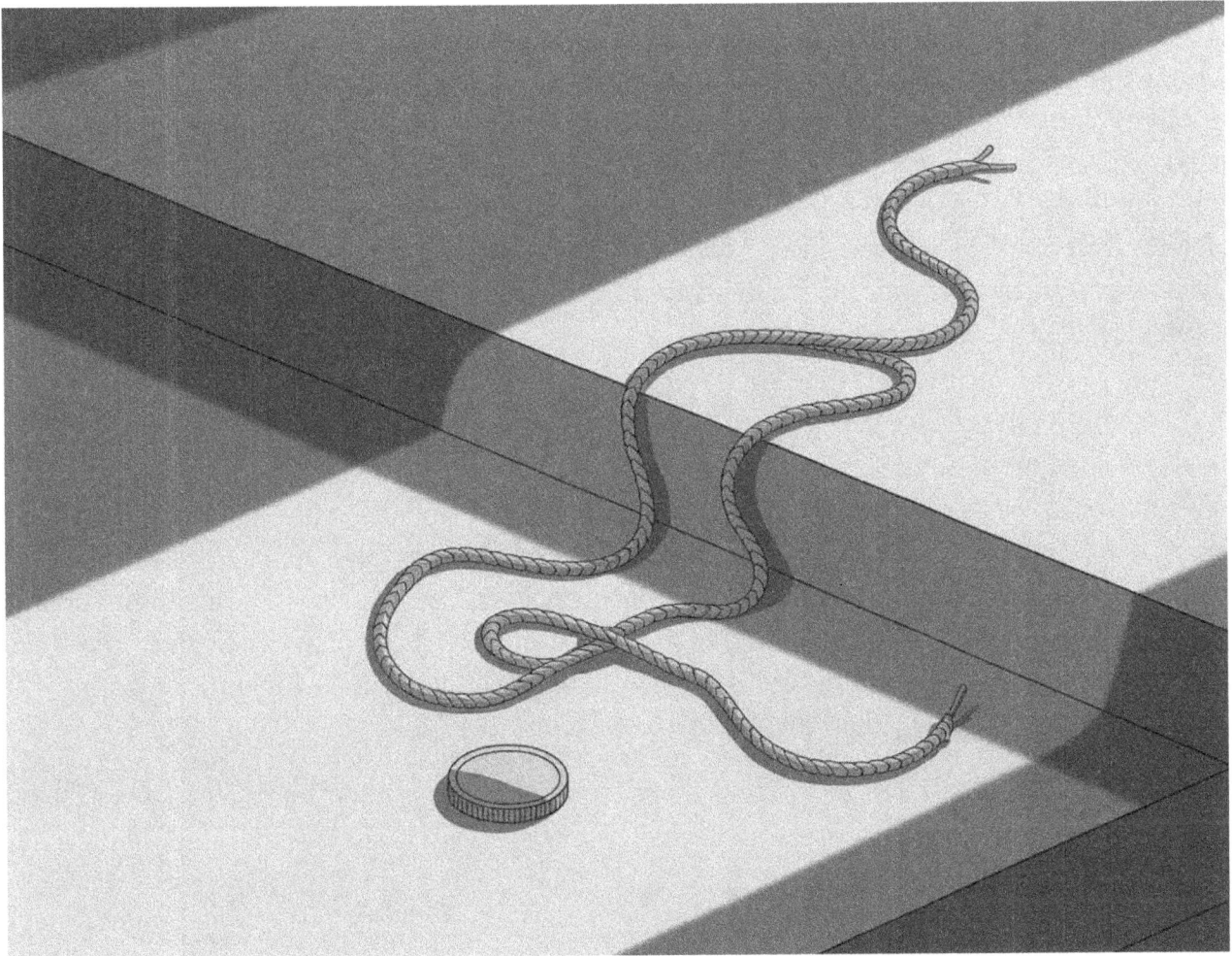

Starting the investment process can be both thrilling and a bit daunting, especially when financial resources are tight. The allure of potential gains might lead you to make hasty decisions that could result in significant losses if you don't have a solid strategy in place. Many new investors jump into the market without setting clear financial goals, which can make the journey enjoyable but may also cause you to lose focus or efficiency. By establishing specific objectives, you create a roadmap that provides the guidance and motivation needed to keep your efforts directed and meaningful.

A well-crafted plan is essential. It should clearly outline your financial objectives, risk tolerance, and the steps you'll take to achieve your goals. Without this framework, you might find yourself chasing fleeting market trends or investing in assets without fully grasping their fundamentals. Taking the time to conduct thorough research before making any investment is crucial. Understanding the asset's characteristics, analyzing market conditions, and identifying potential risks are all important steps. Dedicating time to educate yourself can help you make informed choices and avoid pitfalls.

Diversification is a key strategy for managing risk. Concentrating all your investments in a single asset or sector can increase your vulnerability to losses if that area underperforms. By spreading your investments across various asset classes and sectors, you can lessen the impact of any single decline on your overall portfolio. This approach not only helps manage risk but also opens up opportunities for growth in different markets.

It's common for new investors to fall into the trap of making emotional decisions. Feeling anxious during market downturns or overly optimistic during highs is perfectly normal, but allowing emotions to dictate your choices can be counterproductive. Panic selling during a dip or buying at a peak out of fear of missing out often leads to losses. To maintain discipline, consider setting entry and exit points for your investments in advance. Sticking to these predetermined points can help you adhere to your plan and avoid making decisions based on short-term market fluctuations.

Understanding the fees and expenses associated with investing is also vital. High costs can chip away at your returns over time, so it's important to be aware of the charges from your brokerage or investment platform. These may include:

- Account maintenance fees
- Trading commissions
- Other hidden costs

Keeping these expenses in check can enhance your overall returns.

Having realistic expectations is crucial for long-term success. Building wealth is a journey that takes time, and expecting quick profits can lead to disappointment and impulsive decisions. Embrace the fact that investing requires patience and a long-term perspective. By focusing on your primary goals and remaining patient, you can avoid making hasty moves.

Recognizing and Managing Emotional Investment Traps

Emotions play a significant role in investing, sometimes motivating action and at other times making it challenging to make sound decisions. Recognizing and managing these emotional pitfalls is key to making rational choices. Begin by identifying specific triggers—such as **fear**, **greed**, and **overconfidence**—that can lead to impulsive behavior and cloud your judgment, steering you away from your long-term financial goals.

Fear often takes hold during times of market volatility. When markets decline, many investors react by selling off assets to avoid further losses. This instinctive response can lock in losses instead of allowing investments the opportunity to recover. Developing a comprehensive strategy with clearly defined entry and exit points can help counteract fear. Sticking to this plan, regardless of market fluctuations, supports rational decision-making and helps you avoid reacting to short-term changes.

Greed can drive individuals toward high-risk investments in the quest for quick gains, often resulting in taking on more risk than is wise. Setting realistic expectations for returns and building a diversified portfolio can help keep this emotion in check. Diversification spreads investments across various asset classes, reducing the impact if one underperforms. A balanced approach allows for effective risk management and helps curb the urge to chase speculative opportunities.

Overconfidence is another common trap, leading to excessive trading or overlooking important market signals. This often arises from an inflated sense of one's own market knowledge. Practicing humility by regularly reviewing and adjusting your investment plan based on data and professional advice keeps your decisions grounded in objective analysis rather than an overestimation of your abilities.

Practical techniques can help maintain rationality and navigate emotional traps. Consider the following strategies:

- Engage in mindfulness practices to reduce stress and assist in regulating emotions.
- Schedule regular portfolio reviews to prevent impulsive reactions to market changes.
- Utilize automation tools like stop-loss orders to enforce discipline by automatically selling an asset when it reaches a certain price, protecting against significant losses.

A long-term perspective on investing helps maintain focus on gradual wealth accumulation rather than reacting to short-term market swings. Connecting with a supportive network or finding a mentor can provide valuable guidance and accountability, keeping you on track. Expanding your knowledge of *behavioral finance* deepens your understanding of how emotions influence decisions, making it easier to recognize and address these effects.

Cognitive biases such as **anchoring** and **confirmation bias** can significantly influence choices. Anchoring occurs when you fixate on a specific detail, like the purchase price of a stock, allowing it to sway your decisions too much. Confirmation bias leads you to seek out information that supports your existing beliefs while ignoring contrary evidence. To counter these biases, seek out different perspectives and critically evaluate your assumptions. This approach fosters a more complete understanding and leads to better-informed decisions.

Staying Calm and Confident in Volatile Markets

Common Mistake

One of the most frequent mistakes new investors make is reacting impulsively to market volatility. Letting fear or excitement drive your decisions can lead to buying high and selling low, which undermines long-term growth. Instead, focus on your strategy, use waiting periods before acting, and remember that volatility is normal. Staying calm and informed helps you avoid costly errors and build wealth steadily, even with small amounts.

Investing can often seem complex, especially during times of market volatility. However, having a solid understanding of trends and economic indicators can really empower you to interpret fluctuations with greater accuracy and confidence. This knowledge helps demystify the seemingly erratic behavior of financial markets and equips you with the tools to make decisions that align with your long-term goals.

Start by making it a habit to follow financial news from trustworthy sources. Established newspapers, credible online platforms, and informative podcasts that provide daily or weekly updates on market conditions are all excellent resources. Staying informed allows you to identify potential triggers for changes, such as:

- Shifts in interest rates
- Significant geopolitical events
- Evolving consumer behavior

With these insights, you can better anticipate movements and adjust your investment strategy as needed.

Reviewing historical data is also essential for understanding market behavior. By looking at past events, you can uncover recurring patterns and trends. For example, examining how markets reacted during previous economic downturns or growth periods offers valuable context for current events, making them feel less unpredictable. This perspective helps you recognize that **volatility** is a normal part of investing and not always a cause for concern.

To enhance your understanding of investment principles and dynamics, take advantage of financial education resources. Online courses, webinars, and workshops provide structured learning on topics ranging from basic strategies to advanced analysis. These tools help you build a solid foundation, making it easier to interpret complex signals and make informed choices.

Regularly reviewing your strategy is vital for managing market volatility. Evaluating your portfolio in light of new information keeps it aligned with your long-term goals and risk tolerance. This proactive approach ensures your plan remains current and helps you stay focused on your objectives, reducing the likelihood of emotional reactions to short-term fluctuations.

Practicing with simulations or trading platforms can also be a great way to gain experience in handling volatility without risking real money. These tools allow you to test different strategies and observe how they perform under various conditions. Simulating real-world scenarios builds your confidence and encourages a more disciplined approach to investing.

Remember, the goal isn't to predict the market with perfect accuracy—even seasoned investors find that challenging. Instead, focus on developing the knowledge and skills needed to navigate the ups and downs with a sense of calm. Understanding what drives market movements and honing your analytical skills can transform **volatility** from a source of stress into an opportunity for growth and learning.

Stress-reduction techniques, such as **mindfulness** and **meditation**, can significantly enhance your ability to remain calm and composed during times of market volatility. Dedicating just 10 to 15 minutes each day to these practices helps train your mind to stay present and manage anxiety effectively. This approach paves the way for clearer investment decisions, minimizing the chances of impulsive actions driven by panic.

Creating a personal action plan for volatile periods is also a valuable strategy. It should outline specific steps to take when emotions run high. For example, you might choose to implement a **24-hour waiting period** before making any financial decisions. This pause allows you to evaluate the situation more objectively and avoid hasty choices. Reaching out to a trusted financial advisor during these times can provide valuable insights and guidance, helping you make informed decisions based on expert analysis.

Engaging in physical exercise and maintaining healthy lifestyle habits are essential for emotional regulation. Regular activities like jogging, yoga, or brisk walking for at least 30 minutes three times a week can release endorphins, naturally boosting your mood and reducing stress. Additionally, eating a balanced diet rich in whole foods and ensuring you get 7 to 9 hours of quality sleep each night are key factors that contribute to emotional stability.

Setting up automated alerts for significant market movements can help you stay informed without the need for constant monitoring. Consider the following criteria for alerts:

- A 2% change in major indices
- Specific stock prices reaching a predetermined level
- Other significant market events

These notifications enable thoughtful responses to important shifts, allowing you to make decisions based on data rather than emotions. Having a reliable system in place ensures you receive timely information and can act with a clear mind.

A support network of fellow investors adds another layer of resilience. Sharing experiences and strategies with others fosters a sense of community and helps alleviate feelings of isolation during challenging times. Connecting with like-minded individuals offers opportunities to exchange insights, learn from one another, and gain new perspectives, which can provide reassurance and help you stay grounded when markets are turbulent.

Continuing your education about the psychological aspects of investing is also vital. Understanding how emotions influence decision-making equips you with the tools to recognize and manage these effects more effectively. Expanding your knowledge of *behavioral finance* deepens your awareness of cognitive biases that may impact your choices and introduces techniques to counteract them.

Chapter 13: Next Steps for Long-Term Investing Success

A long-term investment strategy requires a thoughtful plan that aligns with your unique financial goals. The first step is to set clear, measurable objectives that reflect your individual situation. Whether you're aiming for a comfortable retirement, saving for a down payment on a home, or planning for future educational expenses, defining specific targets will guide your decisions and help you maintain focus.

Start by utilizing financial calculators to estimate the future value of your investments. These handy tools can show you how much you need to contribute regularly to reach your goals. For instance, if your target is to accumulate **$500,000** for retirement over 30 years, a financial calculator can help you determine the monthly contributions needed based on your chosen rate of return. This method provides a solid plan and clarifies the steps necessary to achieve your financial aspirations.

Diversification is a key element of a strong investment approach. By spreading your assets across various classes—such as equities, fixed income, real estate, and mutual funds—you can reduce risk and enhance potential returns. Each asset class reacts differently to market changes, so a diversified portfolio can help cushion against volatility. For example, when equities may not perform well, fixed income investments can offer stability, while real estate might present growth opportunities. The goal is to create a mix that aligns with your risk tolerance and financial dreams.

A **buy-and-hold strategy** also supports long-term investing. This approach involves purchasing investments and holding onto them for many years, allowing you to benefit from the power of compound growth. Compound interest plays a significant role in building wealth, as your returns generate additional earnings over time. For example, investing **$10,000** at an annual return of **7%** could grow to about **$76,123** in 30 years due to compounding.

Regularly reviewing your portfolio and making adjustments is essential to keep it aligned with your evolving financial goals and risk tolerance. Life events can change your circumstances and may require you to update your investment strategy. As you near retirement, you might consider shifting toward more conservative investments to protect your capital, while earlier in your career, a more aggressive strategy could help maximize growth.

Stay informed about changes in tax laws and retirement account regulations, as these factors can significantly influence your strategy. Understanding the tax implications of different accounts, such as *Roth IRAs* or *401(k)s*, empowers you to make informed decisions about where to allocate your funds. Being aware of updates to contribution limits or withdrawal rules ensures you can fully benefit from these accounts.

You might also consider incorporating sustainable and ethical investing principles into your strategy. If these values resonate with you, evaluate companies based on their environmental, social, and governance (*ESG*) practices. Choosing firms that prioritize sustainability and ethical governance can align your portfolio with your beliefs and may also lead to strong returns. Research indicates that companies with robust *ESG* practices often carry lower risk and achieve better long-term performance.

To cultivate lifelong learning and investment habits, it's essential to prioritize ongoing financial education. Begin by exploring a variety of resources, such as **"The Intelligent Investor"** by Benjamin Graham, reputable webinars led by financial experts, and engaging blogs or podcasts that focus on long-term strategies. These materials offer valuable insights into market trends, investment techniques, and key economic indicators, empowering you to make informed decisions. Aim to read at least one investment-related book each month and participate in a webinar each quarter to keep your knowledge fresh and relevant.

Connecting with a community of like-minded individuals can significantly enhance your educational journey. Investment clubs and online forums provide wonderful opportunities to share insights, discuss strategies, and learn from the real-world experiences of others. These interactions can introduce you to diverse perspectives and exciting opportunities you might not discover on your own. Seek out local meetups or online groups that resonate with your specific interests and goals. Establishing a consistent routine for reviewing your portfolio is vital for achieving long-term success. Dedicate a specific time each week to:

- Assess your current holdings
- Evaluate their performance
- Explore potential new investments

This habit keeps you informed and helps you identify areas that may need adjustments. Consider using a spreadsheet or investment tracking app to organize your data and simplify the review process.

A structured savings plan is fundamental to effective investing. Setting up automatic contributions to your accounts ensures steady capital growth. Arrange for automatic transfers from your checking account to your investment accounts to build your portfolio consistently and minimize the temptation to spend money that could be invested for future growth.

Utilizing financial management tools can help you monitor spending and identify areas for savings. Budgeting apps or software allow you to categorize expenses and analyze your habits. This process can uncover opportunities to reduce discretionary spending and redirect those funds into investments. For instance, if you notice a monthly dining expense of *$100*, consider trimming that amount and investing the difference.

Regular reminders for portfolio rebalancing are essential to maintain your desired asset allocation. Over time, different asset classes may perform differently, causing your allocation to drift from your original plan. Rebalancing involves adjusting your holdings to return to your target allocation, keeping your portfolio diversified and aligned with your risk tolerance. Aim to rebalance at least once a year or whenever your allocation shifts by more than **5%** from your target.

A mindset of patience and resilience is crucial for navigating market fluctuations. Understand that volatility is a normal part of investing, and long-term success often requires weathering short-term downturns. Stay focused on your long-term goals and adhere to your strategy, even during challenging times. Mindfulness and stress-reduction techniques can help you remain calm and centered during these periods.

Chapter 14: Frequently Asked Questions for Beginners

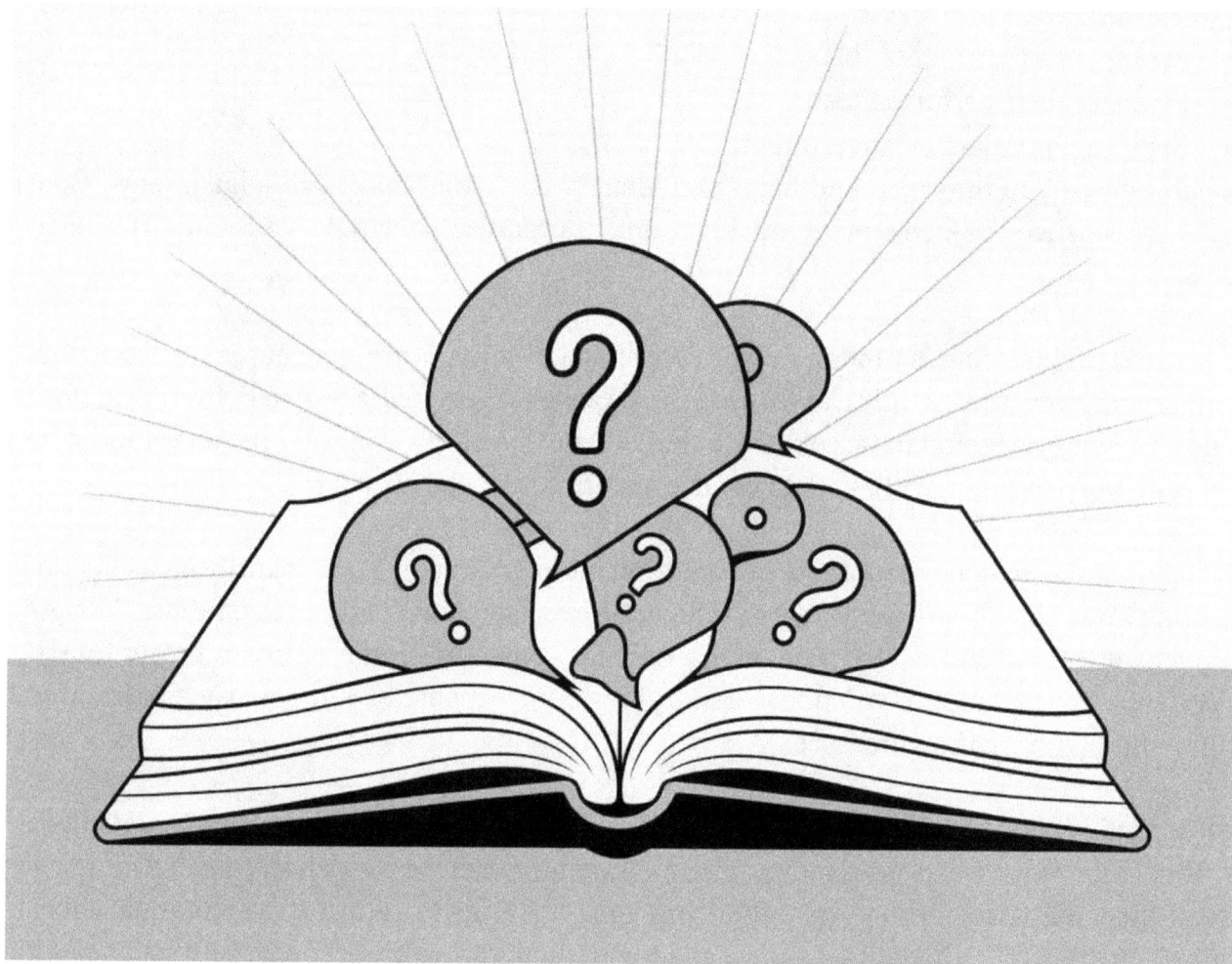

Investing is a thoughtful way to build wealth over time, and grasping its basic principles is essential for anyone looking to secure their financial future. At its core, investing means putting money into various financial instruments with the aim of earning a measurable return. This approach is vital for growing wealth because it allows your funds to increase at rates that often exceed those of traditional savings accounts, primarily due to the higher potential returns from different asset classes.

Many people mistakenly think that investing is only for the wealthy or that it resembles gambling. In reality, it is accessible to individuals from all financial backgrounds and is fundamentally different from gambling. While gambling often relies on luck, investing is about making informed choices based on careful research and analysis. Understanding the relationship between **risk** and **return** is crucial for making decisions that align with your financial goals and comfort level with risk.

A few key terms can help clarify the basics:

- Stocks represent ownership in a company, so when you buy one, you become a shareholder with a claim on part of the company's assets and earnings.
- Bonds are loans made to corporations or governments, and you receive regular interest payments along with the bond's face value when it matures.
- Mutual funds pool money from many investors to buy a diversified mix of stocks, bonds, or other securities, all managed by professionals.
- Exchange-Traded Funds (ETFs) work similarly to mutual funds but are traded on stock exchanges like individual stocks, offering more flexibility and often lower fees.

Risk and **return** are foundational concepts in investing. Generally, higher potential returns come with greater risk. Knowing your risk tolerance—how much risk you're willing and able to take—is key to making informed choices. For example, if you prefer less risk, you might opt for bonds or conservative mutual funds that focus on preserving capital. If you're comfortable with more risk in hopes of higher returns, you might consider investing in stocks or growth-focused ETFs.

The power of **compounding** is one of the most appealing aspects of investing. When returns start generating their own returns, your wealth can grow much faster. For instance, investing $100 at a 5% annual return gives you $105 after one year. In the second year, your return is calculated on $105, not just the original $100. Over time, this effect can significantly enhance your wealth, even if you invest small amounts regularly.

Getting started with investing, even with a small amount, is easier now than ever before. The first step is to open an investment account. You can choose a brokerage account for flexible trading or a retirement account like an IRA or 401(k) for tax benefits on long-term savings. Many platforms and apps now support micro-investing, allowing you to begin with as little as $5. These services typically offer user-friendly interfaces, low fees, and educational tools to help you make informed choices.

Setting up automatic contributions can help you build an investing habit. Even small, regular deposits can accumulate over time, thanks to compounding. This approach encourages a disciplined attitude toward saving and investing.

Diversification is key to managing investment risk. Spreading your money across different asset classes and sectors helps protect your portfolio if one investment performs poorly. For example, if you invest all your funds in technology stocks and that sector declines, your entire portfolio could suffer. Including bonds, real estate, or other sectors can help limit potential losses.

Index funds and ETFs make it easy to diversify, even with limited resources. These funds track specific indices, such as the S&P 500, and provide access to a broad range of assets. This approach reduces risk and simplifies the investment process, since you don't have to pick individual stocks or bonds.

Beginner investors often use strategies like:

- Dollar-cost averaging: You invest a fixed amount on a regular schedule, regardless of market conditions. This can help smooth out the effects of market fluctuations and may lower your average cost over time.
- Buy-and-hold: This strategy involves purchasing investments and keeping them for the long term, allowing you to benefit from market growth and compounding.
- Growth investing: This focuses on identifying companies with strong potential for future expansion, which can lead to significant returns.

Monitoring your investments and making adjustments as needed is vital for long-term success. Regularly reviewing your portfolio ensures that your investments stay aligned with your goals and risk tolerance. **Rebalancing**—adjusting your asset mix—helps maintain your preferred risk level. It's important to avoid making decisions based on short-term market swings and to stay focused on your long-term plan.

New investors often have concerns about losing money, market downturns, and recessions. These worries are completely understandable, but history shows that markets tend to recover over time. You don't need a financial advisor or a large amount of money to get started; with the right knowledge and tools, anyone can begin investing.

Overcoming Common New Investor Concerns

Fear of losing money is a common concern for new investors, and it's important to understand that market fluctuations are a natural part of the investment journey. The stock market, like other financial markets, experiences ups and downs; however, historical data shows that it typically recovers over time. For instance, after the 2008 financial crisis, the market faced significant declines but eventually bounced back, with many who embraced a long-term strategy seeing impressive growth in their portfolios. This historical resilience underscores the value of **patience** and a **long-term perspective** when making investment choices.

Diversification is essential for reducing the risks tied to market volatility. By spreading investments across various asset classes—such as stocks, bonds, and real estate—you can help cushion the impact of a downturn in any one sector. This strategy acts as a protective measure, safeguarding your portfolio from major losses. For those just starting out, beginning with a small investment can help build confidence gradually, allowing you to acclimate to the market's fluctuations without putting a large portion of your savings at risk.

New investors may find it challenging to select the right options, but a structured approach can make this process easier. Follow these steps:

- Conduct thorough research on potential investments, focusing on key company fundamentals like revenue growth, profit margins, and overall growth potential.
- Investigate industry trends to identify which sectors might thrive in the future.
- Ensure your choices align with your personal financial goals.

For beginners, broad-market index funds or exchange-traded funds (ETFs) are excellent options, as they provide built-in diversification and generally carry less risk than individual stocks.

Feeling overwhelmed by a lack of knowledge is common, but remember that learning about investing is a continuous journey. Utilize free, reputable online resources such as financial news websites, educational platforms, and investment courses to enhance your understanding. Joining investment communities or forums can connect you with peers for support and advice, creating a space to ask questions and share experiences. Building a foundation in basic financial concepts and staying informed about market trends will empower you to make more informed decisions.

Concerns about market crashes and economic downturns are completely valid, and history demonstrates that markets have bounced back from tough times. **Dollar-cost averaging** is a helpful strategy for managing volatility; by investing a fixed amount at regular intervals, you buy more shares when prices are low and fewer when prices are high, which can help lower your average cost over time. Maintaining an emergency fund also provides a financial cushion during challenging economic periods, so you won't need to sell investments at a loss.

Investment terminology can seem daunting, but breaking down these terms can make them more approachable. A glossary of key terms and their definitions can help clear up confusion, and real-world examples can make complex ideas more relatable. Whenever you're uncertain, don't hesitate to seek clarification from trustworthy sources.

Many people worry about how much money they need to start investing, but beginning with a small amount is absolutely fine. What truly matters is making regular contributions, as small, consistent investments can accumulate over time thanks to **compounding**. Micro-investing platforms allow you to start with very little, helping you take those first steps as an investor.

Market timing can often create anxiety for newcomers, and trying to predict the market can lead to emotional decisions and missed opportunities. Instead, focus on a steady investment plan. Setting up automatic contributions helps you resist the urge to time the market and ensures you keep investing regularly. The duration of your investment matters more than trying to guess market movements.

Skepticism about investment apps and digital tools is understandable, yet these resources can be incredibly beneficial. Look for platforms that comply with regulations and read user reviews to find trustworthy options. Digital tools offer convenience, cost savings, and personalized investment advice, making them valuable for those new to investing.

Chapter 15: Take Your First Step Toward Investing Today

Starting your investment journey today is one of the most significant steps you can take for your financial future. The earlier you start, the more time your investments have to grow and benefit from the power of **compounding**. This is when the returns on your investments begin to generate their own returns, creating a snowball effect that can significantly enhance your wealth. For example, if you invest $100 at a 5% annual return, you'll have $105 after one year. In the next year, your return is calculated on $105, not just the original $100, which accelerates your growth over time. This example highlights the importance of starting your investment strategy now, even if you can only begin with a small amount.

To kick things off, open a **brokerage account**. This account is your gateway to the investment world, allowing you to buy and sell financial instruments like stocks, bonds, and exchange-traded funds (ETFs). Many online platforms offer user-friendly interfaces and low transaction fees, making them ideal for beginners. When selecting a service, think about factors such as:

- Account minimums
- Commission fees
- Availability of educational resources

Robinhood, **E*TRADE**, and **Fidelity** are popular options, each offering unique features to cater to different investor needs.

Once your brokerage account is set up, consider choosing a **micro-investing platform** that allows you to invest with very little capital—sometimes as little as $5. These services often round up your everyday purchases to the nearest dollar and invest the spare change into a diversified portfolio. This approach makes investing accessible and helps you develop a consistent habit of saving and investing. *Acorns* and *Stash* are two well-known micro-investing platforms that provide a variety of options and educational tools to support you along the way.

As you embark on your investment journey, it's important to set your personal financial goals by identifying both short-term and long-term objectives. Short-term goals might include saving for a vacation or a new gadget, while long-term goals could focus on building a retirement fund or purchasing a home. Having clear goals keeps you focused and motivated, providing a solid framework for making investment decisions. To align your investments with these goals, consider your risk tolerance, investment timeline, and overall financial situation. For instance, if you prefer a more conservative approach and have a shorter investment horizon, you might opt for safer choices like bonds or dividend-paying stocks.

Creating a simple investment plan that fits your budget is essential for achieving your financial goals. Determine how much you can invest each month by evaluating your income, expenses, and savings. Even small, regular contributions can grow over time thanks to compounding. Budgeting apps or software can assist you in tracking your spending and identifying areas where you can cut back, freeing up more money for investing. Once you have a clear understanding of your finances, diversify your investments across different asset classes to build a balanced portfolio that aligns with your goals and risk tolerance.

Sticking to a regular investment schedule is a wonderful way to build wealth, even if you start with small amounts. The key is to cultivate a consistent habit, which can be easily achieved by setting up **automatic transfers** to your investment account. This approach simplifies the process and ensures you regularly set aside money for your financial future. Over time, these steady contributions can accumulate and grow through the power of **compounding interest**. Achieving financial success requires ongoing effort and patience, as investments often need time to yield results. With a long-term outlook, your assets have the potential to grow significantly.

A supportive environment is essential for keeping you motivated and committed. Connecting with individuals who share your financial goals can foster a sense of community and encouragement. You might consider joining investment clubs or online forums to share experiences, ask questions, and learn from others. These networks provide valuable perspectives and support, helping you stay focused on your objectives.

Having an accountability partner or mentor can further enhance your investment journey. This person can offer guidance, motivation, and practical advice to help you stay on track. An experienced mentor can share insights into market trends and strategies, while an accountability partner can help you stick to your regular investment plan. Together, these relationships create a strong support system that encourages growth and learning.

Learning about investing is a continuous journey, and staying informed about strategies and market trends is crucial for making sound financial choices. As your confidence grows, you may want to explore more advanced topics and tools, such as:

- Different asset classes
- Market indicators
- New platforms

Expanding your knowledge empowers you to adjust your strategies as the market evolves and make better-informed decisions.

The ability to respond to new information and market shifts is vital for any investor. The financial world is always changing, so being able to adapt your approach helps you navigate these shifts successfully. You might need to:

- Rebalance your portfolio
- Explore new options
- Adjust your risk tolerance

Staying flexible and open to change can significantly impact your ability to grow your wealth over time.